THE STORY OF WALL STREET

WALL STREET TODAY

THE STORY OF
WALL STREET

By

ROBERT IRVING WARSHOW

NEW YORK

GREENBERG · PUBLISHER

PRINTED IN THE UNITED STATES OF AMERICA
BY THE VAIL-BALLOU PRESS, INC., BINGHAMTON, N. Y.

For My Mother

The students of history who hold, with Carlyle, that it is chiefly the record of the work of a few great men, will doubtless find in the annals of Wall Street evidence to support their theory. Leadership is nowhere more pronounced than in the New York stock market. Nowhere is it more effective in achieving results. The market is made by the great army of investors and speculators, not by the few brilliant manipulators. But the few contrive all of the sensations—almost all of the great schemes through which fortunes accumulated in ordinary business channels are deftly withdrawn from the original owners by the operator's art.

EDMUND CLARENCE STEDMAN.

CONTENTS

ILLUSTRATIONS

ILLUSTRATIONS

PREFACE

The spirit of enterprise is nowhere so highly regarded or so richly rewarded, as in the United States. Whatever stigma may philosophically be attached to the "mad union of the spirit of enterprise and the greed for gold," there is no denying that its application has been productive of material results which awe by their magnitude and reflect admiration by their magnificence.

We are not here concerned with political implications or philosophical equalities. Beyond that, we see a picture of a consummate industrial order delivered of the unconscious yearning for distinction of myriads of persons working, for individual profit, to a common end. This magnificent organization, reaching from one end of the country to the other is inextricably bound up with the daily happenings of the financial heart of the country, which, though it is more important than any State, we have become accustomed to call by the name of a street. It is Wall Street which mirrors the financial progress of the nation, and the men of Wall Street who share largely in its development.

This book is the story of those men and the events around which their activities center. It is the story of the leaders of the millions who follow the quotations; the men who make them. They have done this, sometimes by good judgment in anticipation, sometimes by forced manipulation, sometimes by accident. But always in action, always in battle. And it is this steady contest, carried on with progressive magnitude and cunning, which makes our story the more interesting in material.

Wall street is a vital and a living organism. As important as it is from the economic viewpoint, so is it interesting from the human side. The generals are seldom more important than the engagements but their story is often the more fascinating. Capital, earnings, trends, cycles, fluctuations and returns are reserved for the statistician. In this story we deal more closely with the men behind the figures and the minds behind the battle.

If this volume treats in what seems an undue proportion with the speculator and the trader, it is not because less importance is attached to the everyday activities of a central money market and exchange. The function of Wall Street as a distributor of risks and a stabilizer of quoted values has been sufficiently and competently treated. This book is more concerned with the startling successes and dramatic failures of those titans who, like the adventurers of the Middle Ages, struck out into original enterprises and uncharted manipulations. It is their plans, their struggles, their successes and failures, with which we are concerned. Whatever the motives, their activities, if not entirely commendable, were always interesting.

THE STORY OF WALL STREET

CHAPTER I

A N area of conflict is the best field for the speculator and no condition more fertile for operations than uncertainty. The American Revolution, with its crude financing methods, which made
every soldier and every tradesman an involuntary investor in the securities of the governing bodies, made
the first opportunity for speculation on a large scale in
the United States.

The credit problem of the revolutionary government
was a serious one. There were cool minds among the
leaders, men with innate financial sagacity like Robert
Morris and Alexander Hamilton, who felt that direct
taxation was the soundest method of raising the large
proportion of the necessary war funds. But a people
roused to a fighting pitch by unfair taxation could not
be expected to react favorably to any such method. It
might be financially prudent but politically it was un-
wise. In such a time, the easiest method is usually the
practicable method. The printing of money and the issuance of securities and other evidences of debt is the
most painless form of tiding over a war period. In this

case it was generously used, not only by the Federal Government but by the local and State bodies. The result was a tremendous amount of paper, both money and scrip, of fluctuating and little value, held by thousands of persons unacquainted with their value. When the Revolution came to an end, the soldiers received back-pay and a bonus in a generous amount, but in scrip. Back of all this paper was only the possibility of redemption by the Government when it became solvent. For a few years after the end of the war, there was little talk of redemption. The soldiers went back to their trades and their farms, entered into their daily routine, and after vainly trying to pass on their worthless paper, resigned themselves to their loss. "Not worth a continental," became a popular phrase, and the same could be said, in varying degree, of the mass of other paper issued by the States and the Continental Government.

Soon after Alexander Hamilton became Secretary of the Treasury, it became rumored among the politicians and wealthy merchants in the large cities of the East that there would be an effort made to push through Congress a bill to redeem all government securities and certificates at par. Many of these men, politicians made and speculators born, saw possibilities of a grand operation. In the interior cities this paper, being worthless in circulation, was considered worthless in value. The rumors of redemption were discreetly verified by the moneyed interests, and several independent groups

WALL STREET IN 1784

*Showing John Simmons and his well known tavern, the gathering
place for the leading merchants of the day.*

proceeded to capitalize on their inside information. News was slow to travel in those times, and even after Hamilton's Report for Redemption had been read in the Senate, the information was not for months conveyed to the interior. Under such conditions, the possibilities for plunder and profit were tremendous.

Hamilton had been announced for appointment in September, 1789. Before the end of the year three separate syndicates had been formed in New York, Philadelphia and Boston, to buy up all available paper at greatly depreciated prices, in anticipation of redemption. One member of Congress, in the confidence of Hamilton, chartered two fast sailing vessels, which immediately started South, armed with ready cash and intent on gobbling up all the paper in sight. It was not long before the original holders, the soldiers, farmers and merchants, who had received the scrip from the government, were left with little cash, and the securities were centered in the large cities. The syndicates, composed in the main of wealthy individuals allied with members of Congress, were holding for a rise.

There is little evidence of any connivance by Hamilton in this situation. He believed in the soundness of his plans, and the speculative juggling made possible by these plans he would not permit to deter him from his final objective.

Whatever Hamilton's part in it, there is no question that his financial plans for the new government were directly responsible for this organized speculation, which in its result defrauded thousands of small holders to the benefit of a few influential persons in Hamilton's confidence.

In January, 1790, the House and Senate received Hamilton's "Report." One part of it called for the funding of all government securities at par; another called for the assumption by the government of the State debts. The actual reading of the "Report" was the signal for a fresh offensive by the organized syndicates to corner all the paper at depreciated prices, and led also to the formation of new groups, which, not having been in Hamilton's confidence, had not been previously apprised of the proposed redemption. Even at this stage the holders in the interior, not in touch with the large cities, had no idea of the appreciation in value of their paper, and it was not a difficult task for the speculators to purchase quantities of certificates at fifteen to twenty cents on the dollar.

The "Report" was received by some of the legislators with great surprise; not so by the speculators who filled the galleries and overflowed into the lobbies. Senator Maclay wrote in his journal that "it occasioned many serious faces," and he himself "was struck of a heap." Complaints were heard among the legislative representatives who professed democratic leanings, and one comment was that "a committee of speculators in certificates could not have formed it more to their advantage."

The plan was indeed unfair. The proposal to refund the government certificates with bonds at par, and bearing interest, would not only give full return to the speculators buying at lower prices, but would necessitate some form of general taxation to produce the revenue for interest. This taxation would be paid in large part by the very soldiers, farmers, and small merchants who had parted with their paper at a substantial loss. It was an unfair arrangement, but to the audacious Hamilton, who believed in a strong, stable government backed by the large commercial interests, the present unfairness was a minor consideration. He was convinced of the necessity for a strong public credit, and he was resolved to secure it, no matter how powerful the opposition, nor how logical the objections. This immigrant boy from the West Indies, whom Adams called "the bastard brat of a Scotch pedlar," was no believer in democratic government, nor the rights of the masses. Hamilton believed in the rule of gentlemen, and to him the term gentleman meant the cultivated, educated and moneyed group, who made up the aristocracy of the young government. As early as 1794 he wrote to George Washington that he "long since learned to hold public opinion of no value." To this viewpoint, his present plans were entirely consistent.

There were as yet no organized stock exchanges, and most of the transactions in the government certificates were made directly. There was a group of auctioneers at the eastern end of Wall Street, who began to act as agents for the purchase and sale of these securities, although under no organized rules. Not until 1792, when some bank stocks began to be traded in, was any effort made towards the formation of an organized securities exchange.

Meanwhile, in the coffee-houses along Wall Street, the plan of redemption was the main subject of discussion. "I really fear," wrote Maclay, "that the members of Congress are deeper in this business than any others." True it was, for no less distinguished a person than Robert Morris, the chief legislative agent of Hamilton in the Senate, and one of the leaders of the Revolution, was at the head of the largest syndicate organized for the speculation. Fisher Ames, Christopher Gore and Jeremiah Wadsworth, were actively connected with other groups. Indeed, it was Wadsworth, member of Congress from Connecticut, who sent the vessels to the South to attempt to buy up all the available paper there. So persistent were the rumors of inside manipulation that the New York *Daily Advertiser* printed a statement, that should Hamilton's funding plan succeed, Robert Morris would benefit to the extent of $18,000,-000, Jeremiah Wadsworth $9,000,000 and Governor Clinton $5,000,000.

The struggle on the floor of the House against the policy of redemption was stubborn and protracted. Counter plans and compromises were suggested and de-

WALL STREET IN 1789

The large building is the old City Hall, and in the foreground is the famous buttonwood tree under which the early brokers used to meet.

bated. But Hamilton was firm. He was possessed with the one idea of financial stability, whatever the present cost to the masses. He listened to no counter suggestions, brooked no compromise. His powerful party organization howled down objections and, with his legislative machine functioning perfectly, the first part of the 'Report' was adopted. Government securities were to be redeemed and funded and the way was open for the second step—the assumption of State debts. There was great jubilation in the coffee-houses along Wall Street, where the speculators made their headquarters. The original speculative "pools" in the United States had successfully completed their first operation.

II

The next step in Hamilton's program was the assumption of the State debts. The speculative groups held as much of this paper as of government securities, and to complete the coup the second part of the plan must be pushed through. Here there was somewhat greater opposition, for the strong State Governments of the South, whose paper was of real value, objected to the levelling process. The vote was held on March 11th, and Maclay noted that he observed "the rendezvousing of the crew of the Hamilton galley," and that "all hands are piped to quarters." When the vote was taken, there was distress among the Hamilton party. The plan had lost by

[29]

two votes. It seemed a sorry day for the speculators—
they had reams of this paper on their hands, and unless
the vote was reversed, all the previous gains would be
wiped out. But Hamilton had not given up—for him,
it meant merely another battle to win against odds.
For he was a tenacious fighter. Opposition only whet-
ted his appetite for battle, and he made up his mind to
make an issue of his Redemption policy. Once com-
mitted, the stubborn Hamilton decided to sacrifice
whatever other party measures were necessary, to secure
a personal victory.

For the next three months, there were few developments. The "pools" held on to their paper. Some brave
spirits, confident in Hamilton's ability and determination, accumulated even more paper. But things looked
bad.

In June, 1790, Thomas Jefferson, Secretary of State,
arrived in the United States from France. Hamilton had
not been able to swing any more votes to "assumption,"
in spite of all his keen bargaining with the opposition
group. Through Jefferson he achieved his purpose. The
terms were simple. Hamilton needed one vote in the
Senate and five in the House to assure adoption. Jefferson wanted the capital for the South, Hamilton wanted
"assumption." The bargain was made. Whatever the
public thought of the result, Jefferson and Hamilton
both gained politically, and the speculators financially. In Wall Street there was great joy. The

success of the syndicates was complete, and in the words of Maclay, "Speculation wiped a tear from either eye."

III

The result of the redemption policy put into effect by Hamilton was the issuance of public stock, which was in effect the same as the modern government bonds. This new supply of paper soon became the source of a great deal of trading, and the result was a flurry in the business of the auctioneers who were centered around the eastern end of Wall Street. The auctioneers, being the only merchants conducting private sales, handled most of this business. Some enterprising individuals, however, saw the possibility of making money by acting as independent agents, and set up small establishments for dealing in the public stock. This intrusion the auctioneers did not welcome. In March, 1792, the more prominent auctioneers, in an effort to monopolize the trading, opened a public "stock exchange" at No. 22 Wall Street. They were not without rivals, however, in the continued competition for this business. In the meantime, the rival independent agents had begun to exchange quotations. They soon found it more efficient to have regular meetings for the transaction of their business, and gathered daily under a buttonwood tree in front of Nos. 68–70 Wall Street. Their organization prospered, and it was not long before they united in an effort to drive the auctioneering establishments from the field. At a meeting held in Corré's Hotel on March 21, 1792, the buttonwood group resolved to have no dealings with the auctioneers and subscribed to a written agreement covering the terms under which trading was to be done.

The agreement was simple. It called for a uniform commission of one-quarter of one per cent, and it provided that members of the group were to give one another preference in all brokerage transactions. The exclusive nature of the trading was emphasized, and because of this agreement this small group soon had a large proportion of the business, their compactness and aggressiveness having routed the auctioneers from the field. This alliance was the direct forerunner of the present New York Stock Exchange. The arrangement entered into in 1792 was stringently enforced, and served to give these pioneering brokers a virtual monopoly of the stock-trading business. So effective were its provisions, that not until 1817 was any more formal or detailed written agreement considered necessary.

The early trading was mainly in the public stock, although the rapid organization of banks brought about by increasing needs soon brought a new form of security into the market and a greater public participation. Twenty-four individuals or firms met each day under the shade tree in the first year of the organiza-

THE TONTINE COFFEE-HOUSE IN 1797

Erected in 1792 at the corner of Wall and Water Streets, it was for two
generations intimately identified with the business history of the city.

tion. In 1793, what was then the most pretentious business structure on Wall Street was erected, the Tontine Coffee-house. It soon became the commercial center for the business transactions of New York's thirty-five thousand inhabitants, and here the associated brokers established their first official indoor headquarters.

The public interest in stock trading was increasing, a condition which distressed government officials. By 1791 the New York papers had already begun publishing day by day quotations on the government scrip, so immediate was the public's interest. The continuous formation of the new banks to meet the growing commercial needs of the country also stimulated the public's imagination. Just as the industrial mergers in the late nineties of our time served as a signal for widespread public participation in stock trading, so did the rapid organization of new banks from 1790 on stimulate the acquisitive sensibilities of the population. And just as, in our time, the powers tremble at the possibilities of general public speculation and high interest rates, so did the politicians of that day lament the course of events. In a letter from Madison to Jefferson: "Stock and scrip are the sole domestic subjects of conversation . . . speculations carried on with money borrowed at from two-and-a-half per cent a month to one per cent a week. What do you think of the scrip money?" In a letter from Jefferson to Thomas Rutledge: "Ships are lying idle at the wharfs, buildings are stopped, capital withdrawn from commerce, manufacturers, arts, and agriculture to be employed in gambling, and the tide of public prosperity . . . is arrested in its course. . . . I imagine that we shall hear that all the cash has quitted the extremities of the nation and accumulated here."

It seemed to be Alexander Hamilton's mission to furnish fuel for speculative conjectures. For it was his establishment of the National Bank which further stimulated the speculative mania which was sweeping the East. Hamilton was having his way in developing the mercantile interests of the country and the commercial cities were rejoicing. Indeed, the gouty Maclay exactly, if sourly, expressed the state of affairs. "Congress may go home," he wrote in his diary, "for Mr. Hamilton is all-powerful and fails in nothing he attempts."

The organization of the National Bank and the issuance of the National Bank stock were followed by a precipitous rise in its securities. Madison was shocked to find "the members of the Legislature who were most active in pushing this job openly grasping its emoluments." The press became alarmed at the universal speculation. The *Pennsylvania Gazette* wrote that speculators had "turned raving mad, and others so agitated that they appear on the border of insanity." Hamilton himself was very much concerned at the too avid approval of his schemes, at least in the manner it was manifested, and through Fenno, his press representative, urged caution. All sorts of wild rumors were circulated.

In the New York *Daily Advertiser* of August 8, 1791, we find the note that "efforts were being made to buy up all the securities in the city, and for this purpose a powerful combination was formed . . . on Saturday night to reduce the prices." By August 15th, the same paper reversed its opinion. "It has risen like a rocket," wrote the financial editor, talking of the National Bank stock. "Like a rocket it will burst with a crack and down drops the rocket stick. What goes up must come down—so take care of your pate, brother Jonathan."

The steady rise in securities had attracted a large public participation, and the insiders, followers of Hamilton and directors of the bank, who had purchased the stock at original issue prices, found it a good time to dispose of their holdings. As soon as they were out of the market the boom collapsed. The National Bank stock was selling for 195 in August, 1791. Without warning the New York banks, closely connected with the sold-out insiders, stopped discounting for the independent speculators. The bubble burst as quickly as it had formed, and by September the quotations showed at 108. The public was left holding the bag and the bank stock, and the drop was as precipitous as the rise. There was much grumbling and indignation, but the loss remained. Once again the political leaders of the country had made a neat turn.

Members of Congress had profited considerably in this operation. Together with the bankers and the board of directors, they had allotted a great deal of the bank stock to themselves at original prices, and most of them had sold at the top. Their actions did not evade the public notice and the talk of a "corrupt squadron" was common. Jefferson definitely made the charge on the floor of the House, but nothing was ever done about the matter. The political controversy did not affect the brokers' business. The activity in stocks gave the new brokers' organization a bit of a boom, and through it all, the brokers retained the calm detachment from the public's loss which has become a tradition in the Street. Then, as now, no period was so serious, nor the ordinary trading excitement of the day sufficiently diverting as to prevent a few extraneous bets. So we read in the notebook of one of the group who met under the buttonwood tree, these entries: "I bet G. McEvers $10.00 to $5.00 that there would not be 3,000 votes taken at the ensuing election for Governor in the City and County of New York." And again: "I bet Robert Cocks sr., a pair of satin breeches that Jay would be elected Governor by a majority of 500 or more."

A great many persons had lost a great deal of money in this manipulative cycle. They had little to comfort them in the knowledge that the beginning of some of New York's great family fortunes date from this coup. And it is safe to assume that many did not smile with the columnist who followed his admonition to "watch your pate, Jonathan," with his question:

WALL STREET GROWS UP

What magic this among the people
That swells a May pole to a steeple?

IV

Alexander Hamilton's financial plans had succeeded in laying the basis for a solid credit structure. In the process there had been inside manipulations, widespread fraud, and great individual loss. But the effect upon the long-time commercial development of the country was extremely favorable. Contrasted with the primitive trading methods of the pre-Revolutionary days, when there were no banks and no financial exchanges, by 1792 the monetary system had become comparatively well organized. Merchants in need of funds, before Hamilton's financial structure was erected, were forced to borrow from each other. A complicated circulation of currency consisting of guineas, doubloons, pistoles, johannes pieces, and sequins, all of foreign origin, had served to complicate and confuse the simplest transactions. The forcing through of Hamilton's financial program had the result of simplifying business transactions by standardizing and expanding the currency of the country, establishing the credit of the government both here and abroad, and instituting banking facilities for the Eastern merchants.

The National Bank organized by Hamilton was not the first banking institution in the country, but it carried the greatest prestige and served as a stimulus to the rapid growth of the entire banking system. As early as 1780, Robert Morris, then Superintendent of Finance, had organized an institution he called the Pennsylvania Bank. It was a bank only in name, its main purpose being to act as an agent in distributing and transporting supplies for the army. After having done very useful work in this connection, and also in securing the loan of funds for the government, it terminated its existence in 1784.

In 1781, Robert Morris presented to Congress his plan for the establishment of what was to be the first commercial bank in the United States. In December of that year, this bank was chartered under the name of Bank of North America, and immediately began active operations, making its headquarters in a store on the north side of Chestnut Street in Philadelphia. The capital was $400,000, and the government subscribed to 633 shares of the stock at the offering price of $400 a share. That operations were immediately profitable is evidenced by the fact that in January, 1784, there was a new issue of 1,000 shares at $500 a share, an advance of twenty-five per cent in value in about two years.

Philadelphia was then the financial center of the country, and just as it had the first commercial bank, so did it have in time a better organized stock exchange. But New York was growing, and its financial leaders did not delay in following Philadelphia's example in developing

EARLY BANKS IN WALL STREET

*The northeast corner of Wall and William Streets about 1797.
The corner building was occupied by the Bank of New
York; adjoining it is the New York Insurance
Company. The third building housed
the City Bank.*

WALL STREET IN 1834

*A view down the financial center of New York from Trinity
Church. No. 1 Wall Street (the building on the right)
was then occupied by a famous lottery office.*

their financial institutions. On June 9, 1784, the Bank of New York commenced business at No. 67 St. George's Square, now Franklin Square. The capital was $500,000, divided into 1,000 shares. This institution, together with a branch of the National Bank established in New York in 1792, served as a great aid to the merchants as well as speculators. In fact, it was often charged that accommodation was uniformly extended to speculators to the detriment of the merchants. Not having a federal reserve board as yet to curb this tendency, little attention was paid to the protests.

For some time the Bank of New York had a virtual monopoly of the privately operated banking business in New York. Alexander Hamilton was an active member of the board, and because of his political influence, it was well-nigh impossible for any other group to secure a charter from the Legislature. Hamilton's hold on the legislators was so powerful that it was generally recognized that a charter for a new bank was an impossible attainment. Not until the ingenious mind of Aaron Burr devised a plan to secure a charter for a rival bank under another guise, was this monopoly broken and a new institution established. In the spring of 1799 a petition was presented to the Legislature asking for a charter for a company whose purpose was to introduce pure water into the City of New York. A recent epidemic of yellow fever, generally ascribed to the poor water supply, gave this stated purpose a practical plausibility. Apparently only as a matter of form Burr added some additional powers. The capital was $2,000,000, and there was a clause in the petition stating that, as the entire capital might not be required in the beginning, the surplus capital "might be employed in the purchase of public or other stocks, or in any other moneyed transactions or operations not inconsistent with the laws and Constitution of the State of New York." The Legislature passed the bill without realizing the intent of this joker, and the new corporation, under the name of the Manhattan Company, immediately entered business as a rival banking institution to the Bank of New York. After the breaking of the monopoly by the Manhattan Company the resistance to new banks lessened. The bars were down, and as the business was found to be very profitable, by 1803 forty banks had already been organized in the United States.

Along with the steady growth of the mercantile and financial institutions Wall Street gradually changed its physical aspect. The rapid changes and developments in the activities of the commercial district were rapidly being mirrored in the changed appearance of the historic street.

V

Before the Revolution many eminent personages had made their homes in Wall Street. Captain William Kidd, who at that time had not yet taken to pirating on the seas, owned his residence at No. 56 Wall Street. By marriage to a wealthy widow, he had become one of the first landed proprietors of the famous street. He was a leading figure among the slave traders, who made the district their headquarters, but there were not then the present possibilities for plunder, and he soon went out into broader fields. The McEvers and Verplanck mansions were show-places and the presence of the City Hall and Trinity Church on the thoroughfare early established its social prestige. Opposite the City Hall and directly at the head of Broad Street stood the cage, pillory, stocks and whipping post. The Merchants' Coffee-house on the corner of Water Street was the center of the political life of New York, as later, with the changing emphasis of interests, it became the merchants' meeting place. Still earlier, it had been the rendezvous of Captain Kidd and his slave-traders, but the growing social prestige of the inhabitants of the district changed the complexion of its clientele. Indeed the very slave market which had given the coffee-house its initial stimulus as a meeting center was condemned by the later patrons, the influential politicians of the community. The minutes of the Common Council carry this resolution: "Said Meal (Slave) Market greatly obstructs the agreeable prospects of the East River which those that live in Wall Street would Otherwise enjoy; that it Occasions a Dirty Street Offensive to the Inhabitants on each side and Disagreeable to those that pass and Repass to and from the Coffee-house a place of Great Resort." The abolition of the Slave Market removed the last vestige of the old disrepute of Wall Street and led to the settlement there of many more of New York's leading families in pre-Revolutionary days.

During the Revolution, Wall Street was occupied by the enemy, and when the British abandoned it in 1783, it took on the appearance of a deserted village. What few houses remained were empty and the street was occupied mainly by prowling hogs. One of the few remaining buildings, after the British laid waste to the district, was John Simmons's Tavern on the corner of Wall and Nassau, and here a group of men met in February, 1784, to elect James Duane the first American Mayor of New York.

The business life of New York immediately after the Revolution was at a standstill, but the Chamber of Commerce soon began holding meetings at the Merchants' Coffee-house, and in April, 1784, this organization of merchants was duly incorporated by the New York Legislature. The physical revival was slow but steady. The Presbyterian Church was repaired in 1784, and a movement was started to rebuild the ruins of Trinity. The announcement by the Continental Congress that it would make its headquarters in New York gave an impetus to the revival of interest in Wall Street as a center. The Congress was given the use of the City

Hall, and around this building the political and commercial leaders and the lawyers soon made their headquarters. Alexander Hamilton opened his law office at No. 58 (now No. 33) Wall Street, and Aaron Burr settled very near, at No. 10 Cedar Street. Hamilton was a leading figure at the coffee-house, and his work in forcing through ratification of the Constitution by New York State over the opposition of the rural districts made him the hero of the district. This ratification stimulated the confidence of the commercial interests and encouraged a revival in building. In 1788, workmen began to rebuild Trinity Church, and soon after Federal Hall was erected on the northwest corner of Wall and Nassau. It was the most imposing building in New York, and it was on its balcony that Washington was inaugurated. By 1789 Wall Street had definitely displaced Pearl Street as the most important street for New York's thirty thousand inhabitants.

Aaron Burr's Manhattan Company had located at No. 23 Wall Street, and in the next few years the Merchants' Bank was located at No. 25, the United States at No. 38 and the Merchants' at No. 16 Wall Street. The centering of the banks naturally fixed the commercial and speculative center, and from that time on the Street has had no competitor as New York's business headquarters. With the rapid growth of the population land values increased, and the many pretentious private homes were razed to give way to commercial buildings.

Through the early eighteen hundreds, this transforma-
tion continued. The great fire of 1835 which swept the
thoroughfare, put the finishing touches on the former
residential aspect of the Street, for the new buildings
which came up to replace the ruins were, almost without exception, built for business purposes. A writer in
the New York *Mirror* in 1839 noted what is perhaps
still true to-day: "It is as difficult to wend one's way
through Wall Street as it ever was. Physically as well as
financially there is peril in perambulating the street.
Stocks may rise but stones are falling prodigiously in
all directions. The Manhattan and the City Bank are
being torn down, and there are other edifices in Wall
Street under the besom. New York, ever since we knew
it, has been a city of modern ruins—a perfect Baalbeck
of a day's growth and a day's dilapidation. The builder
is abroad one day and is relieved of his labors by the
destroyer the day after. We never expect to see the city
finished, but we have the greatest anxiety to see it
fairly commenced."

VI

Through all of the early period of the industrial and
commercial growth of the United States, the one dominating figure was Alexander Hamilton. It was he who
initiated the plan which established the country's credit
and unified its currency. It was he who originated and

established the first government bank and guided its early growth. Few large-scale industrial ventures were launched which were not first presented for his approval, and no ambitious commercial scheme was formulated without attempting to enlist his support. His impress was on almost every important new venture, and his opinions were used as a barometer both by the commercial and the speculative interests.

It is the more remarkable that this dominating commercial genius should have sprung from so lowly an origin. That he was an illegitimate child was early known in the United States and publicly commented on. That he was, besides, an immigrant could not but militate against him. That he was poor by birth makes all the more remarkable his rise. That he remained poor and died poor, is evidence of his intrinsic honesty in a time when his position made possible the easy accumulation of wealth and the prevailing ethics of the business community did not debar him from such profitable activity.

Hamilton's accomplishments were varied, but in no field was his genius so evident as in his commercial dealings, both in and out of office. By early training, he was a clerk and accountant. His work as a journalist made possible his trip to the States. His gift of oratory and his literary ability, added to his natural talents of leadership, made him one of the great politicians of the Revolution. His academic training was in the law but to his death he believed that he should have been a professional soldier. In all these fields he did well. But it was as an industrial organizer and financier that he accomplished his greatest work. Almost single-handed, he made possible the early commercial independence of the country, and laid the basis for its rapid industrial growth.

Around him there were many men who used his plans for private speculations and his confidence for their personal profit. He knew it and felt it an unavoidable concomitant to the development of his ideas. He was no protector of the masses. The government he desired needed the support of the moneyed groups, and he was determined to advance their interests. That these groups exploited his plans did not concern him so long as they put them into effect. But his personal honesty was unquestioned. To an appeal for funds for charity he was forced to respond: "I wish I were a Croesus; I might then afford solid consolation to these children of adversity, and how delightful it would be to do so. But now, sympathy, kind words, and occasionally a dinner, are all that I can contribute." His term in office as Secretary of the Treasury had made it possible for his friends and political allies to make millions. The fortunes of the Morris family, the Livingstons, the Ellsworths, the Gores, the Schuylers, the Clintons, and the many other Federalists, who were his political allies and in his confidence, date from that period. For himself, he came out of office a poorer man than when he entered. Neither for per-

From the painting by JOHN TRUMBULL *in Boston Museum of Fine Arts*

ALEXANDER HAMILTON, FIRST SECRETARY OF THE TREASURY

He laid the foundation for our whole national financial structure.

sonal profit nor political preferment would he alter or
fail to express his views. Of George Washington, whose
power and importance at that time were second to none,
he wrote: "I find him neither remarkable for delicacy
or good temper . . . for three years past I have felt no
friendship for him and have professed none."

The great influence of Hamilton's genius upon the
commercial development of the country has been recognized by few authorities. This is perhaps due to the
fact that, among his opponents and even among the
members of his own political party, Hamilton was distinctly unpopular. His nature brooked no opposition,
even of a mild type, and his impatience led him to disregard other people's feelings. He was a master in the
planning of abstract problems and their practical ex-
ecution. In the management of men, he was a failure.
It was thus not without cause that men of the reserved
nature of John Quincy Adams and Thomas Jefferson,
irritated by his arbitrary tactics, publicly called him
"bastard." It was Hamilton's inability to regulate his
pace to the men about him that led him finally to the
conclusion that his temperament was not suitable to the
scene of his activities. Toward the close of his life,
thwarted in his later political ambitions by his un-
popularity, he wrote to Morris: "Every day proves to
me more and more that this American world was not
made for me. You, friend Morris, are a native of this
country, but by genius an exotic. You mistake if you

fancy that you are more of a favorite than myself." Hamilton thought in terms of the world, and the men around him thought in terms of the New England town meeting. This difference in viewpoint was to dim his political career, but as a creator of credit agencies and financial institutions, it was to be his greatest aid.

In office Hamilton had organized the country's currency, consolidated its debts and founded a banking system. His Report on Manufactures laid the basis for our present tariff system, and there are few advocates of a protective tariff policy who do not follow Hamilton's line of reasoning to-day. Out of office he was the leading lawyer of his day, and the organizer of the Society of Manufactures, the first large-scale manufacturing venture in the United States. It started operations in Paterson, New Jersey, and was the first industrial organization to sell stock to the general public.

When Hamilton had come into his great influence the commercial interests of the country were laboring under a primitive organization. In 1804, when he died a martyr to the ambitions of Aaron Burr, his traditional rival, he left the country in a favorably advanced form of monetary development. The use of banks had replaced direct borrowing, a stable currency had done away with barter, a protective tariff had made easier the industrial development of the country and secured a national income, while a public Stock Exchange had made it possible to launch and finance large ventures.

WALL STREET GROWS UP

At his funeral every place of business in New York was closed. And among all the varied powers that did him homage, no group was so sincerely distressed, nor left so leaderless, as that part of the cortege which was officially described as "The Chamber of Commerce and Merchants."

CHAPTER II

THE BEGINNING OF LARGE-SCALE ENTERPRISE

POLITICAL shackles can be shed by oratory and physical determination. The more subtle chains of commercial dependence are worn until ability, coupled with organization, gradually file them down. And so it was that for many years after the United States had attained political freedom the country remained a commercial tributary of England. Not until after 1800, when financial stability was forced upon the States by the genius of Alexander Hamilton and Yankee captains of industry began to display the latent American commercial initiative, did the United States begin to take its modest place among the nations of the world.

The steam engine of Watt, the locomotive of Stephenson, and the spinning machinery of Arkwright and Compton, were borrowed from England. Each of these, American inventions improved on what they appropriated. Fulton put the steam engine into a ship and opened a new era of navigation; Howe created the sewing machine; McCormick gave the reaper to the farmer and revolutionized agriculture; Morse contributed the telegraph and made the nation a business unit.

[56]

LARGE-SCALE ENTERPRISE

For every inventor there stood a captain of industry ready to snatch the machine from the workshop, collect the capital to put it in motion, and seek out markets for the flow of goods. They were a race of men new to America and a product of its untrammeled civilization. For the next fifty years the Abbots, Lawrences, Astors, Browns, Vanderbilts, and Brookses of American enterprise were to put American initiative into every corner of the New World. The first quarter of the nineteenth century saw a perfect outbreak of mechanical power appliances in basic industries, and steam, harnessed to the machine, began to substitute the factory for the individual craftsman. The first faint rumblings of the industrial earthquake could be distinguished. The United States was "on the make" as an industrial nation.

Simultaneously with the release of industrial forces, there was a continuous development of new means of communication. In 1807 Fulton's *Clermont* made its first successful trip up the Hudson, and within four years there were four steamboats on the Mississippi. In 1825, the Erie Canal was opened and forged the first link between the West and the Eastern seaboard. The canal made New York the center for the export and import trade of the whole country. Baltimore, then a close rival to New York as industrial center, was hard hit by the diversion of its trade, and at the instigation of Brown Brothers, a leading Baltimore banking firm, the first railroad in the United States was projected as a competitor to New York's advanced transportation facilities. The Baltimore and Ohio Railroad Company was organized with a capital of $5,000,000, and on July 4, 1828, Charles Carroll of Carrollton, the last surviving signer of the Declaration of Independence, laid the cornerstone. A new form of transportation was put into common use and the railroad epoch had begun.

The factories of the country, although enlarged, had not yet become national enterprises and were usually financed locally. The railroads, however, because of the great investment involved, were forced to look for capital from outside sources. From the first, New York banks took a leading part in such financing, as was inevitable from the growing concentration of capital in that city. The banks were also the principal agents for the vast flood of foreign money that poured into the United States for investment in railroad construction—an amount estimated at $400,000,000 during the first fifty years. For the first time, American enterprise began to use national stock distribution as a means of developing large-scale ventures.

With the development of national business enterprises, financed by banks and investors not a part of the management, the services of the banks and the exchanges in New York became of paramount importance. Private banking houses, organized for the purpose of acting as agents in the distribution of railroad securities, now came into being. They helped to give these securities a wide distribution, and stimulated the business of the stock exchanges and other distributing agencies. These were gradually but consistently concentrated in New York, and Wall Street became, without question, the nation's financial capital.

II

The speculative craze following the funding of the national debt had been short-lived. The remorseless manipulative tactics of the political speculators had driven the public to other amusements and the business of the stock brokers was at a low ebb. The newspapers, reflecting this lack of interest, had ceased to print quotations, and not until 1815 was this feature resumed. On March 10, 1815, the New York *Commercial Advertiser* carried the first complete price list of stocks ever published.

PRICE OF STOCKS.

New-York Bank	125	Mutual	110
Manhattan Bank	116 1-2	Globe	102 1-2
Merchants Bank	117 1-2	Washington	116
Mechanics Bank	116 1-2	City Loan	100 1-2
Union Bank	103	Ditto Seven per ct.	104 105
Bank of America	105	Phœnix	
City Bank	110 1-2	Ocean	85
New-York Manuf. Com'y	100	New-York Fireman	
Six per cents. div. off	99		
Louisiana	91		
Three per cents.	55	EXCHANGE.	
Old and Deferred,	95	*Saturday, March 4, 1815.*	
N. York Insurance	00 100	Bills on London, 60 da. 95 96	
Treasury Notes	4 1-4	Amsterdam	
United	90 100	Hamburg	
Eagle, div. off	115	France	

The list contained, as yet, only one manufacturing company. Banks and government securities still monopolized the small amount of trading, although insurance companies had already begun to function and distribute their stock. Not until 1827 did industrials begin to appear in any number, and not until the period of railroad expansion did trading reach any substantial volume. Brokerage was as yet a tame business, for the brokers were then only what their title implied—agents for the purchase and sale of securities. They were not active in trading for their own account and attempted not at all to affect or manipulate security prices. The leaders among them were leaders in the sense of being eminent in their profession as among merchants or bankers. Their trade was profitable but not as yet dramatic. The manipulators had not yet arrived, but the stage was being set for their entrance.

In 1817, the substantial stock brokers of New York comprised eight firms and nineteen individuals. They met daily in the office of Samuel J. Beebe in the old Tontine Coffee-house. The increased business attendant upon the formation of marine and fire insurance companies decided them to prescribe a more detailed organization of their common business and on February 25, 1817, a resolution was passed calling for a new association under the name of the New York Stock and Exchange Board. A set of rules was adopted on May 8th to govern the trading and these rules became the constitution of the board. Officers were elected, and the regulations for admission were definitely prescribed. Commissions were specified for various groups of stocks to vary from ¼ to ½ of one per cent, and for the first time a rule was passed against "wash" sales. On February 21, 1820, a revised constitution was adopted which did not, however, call for any drastic changes.

In its early days the restless members of the board moved about a great deal. In 1819, the yellow fever epidemic forced removal to Washington Hall, at Broadway and Reade Street. In July, 1824, they leased "the lower back room in the rear of the Protection Fire Company" from one Thomas Franklin for three months at an aggregate rental of $100. On March 12, 1825, we find a resolution authorizing the hiring of "Mr. Warren's room for two years, at a rent not exceeding $500," and on May 1, 1827, they moved to still another location on the second story of the newly built Merchants' Exchange Company Building, at Wall and Hanover Streets.

During this period the call started at 11.30 and lasted until all business was completed. Business was not as yet very brisk, and by shortly after one o'clock the brokers usually left for the day. In spite of the limited nature of their activities, the members were already very jealous of their privileges. In 1817, for instance, only one new member was admitted although the files show many applications.

With the public out of the market, the daily proceedings were uneventful. Interest was apathetic, and
contrary to the fevered excitement of our period, every
week saw a new drop in sales volume. Tuesday, March
16, 1830, made the record low mark. On that day only
thirty-one shares were traded in, the dullest day in the
history of the New York Stock Exchange. Twenty-six
shares of United States Bank and five shares of Morris
Canal and Banking Company stock changed hands, and
for the princely sum of $3,470.25 a speculator wishing
to control the day's trading could have bought up all
the stock on the market. Less than a hundred years later,
an average day's trading was more than a hundred thousand times as large.

But this was just a lull before the rise. Soon after,
railroad securities began to appear in the trading, and
the volume increased rapidly and steadily. The Mohawk
and Hudson Railroad, started in August, 1830, was the
first railroad stock to be listed on the Exchange. The
daily trading went along uneventfully and calmly, the
routine punctuated only by a series of further removals
in location, until the panic of 1837 swept the country,
caused the first violent fluctuations in securities and
pushed to the wall some of the leading banking firms in
the country. At such a time men "on the make" find
their best opportunity, and in the volcanic changes
Jacob Little, the first of Wall Street's great line of
manipulators, came to the fore.

CHAPTER III

ENTERPRISE has at no time been so effectively demonstrated as in the early period of railway expansion. So rapidly did American initiative develop this English invention that by 1837 the United States possessed more completed lines and a greater aggregate mileage than any other country. This expansion, rapid, if sometimes chaotic, gave rise to a new type of financier—the manipulative operator. Of this species of Wall Street Jacob Little was the first. Those to follow were to outdo in ingenuity and scope the first of the manipulators, but their methods were largely developed upon his original tactics.

In Jacob Little's time the newspapers had not yet learned the news value of the market leader's activities. There are therefore few facts available covering his exploits. Little learned the game as a clerk with Jacob Barker, a well-known broker in the early '30's. In 1835 he went into business for himself, founding with his brother the firm of Jacob Little and Company. In the panic of 1837 he was a consistent bear, and he thrived on the destruction of values. In this initial campaign, which established him, he invented the idea of the "short" sale.

The pictures we have of him show him a tall, slender, carelessly dressed man, slightly stooped. He was perpetually engaged in speculation. The morning he devoted to cotton and commodities, the afternoon to securities. His interests outside of his beloved speculation were few, and he never left the Street while any one remained to trade. A consistent short seller, he invoked the enmity of his conservative fellow-brokers who were continually engaged in a battle to oust him from the Street. He was curt and cold in his manner, distant in what few associations were necessary to his business. His entire existence revolved around his speculative plans, and so enamored was he of his work that he always delivered in person the stock he had sold and kept all his books and records himself. His operations in the stock market were his work, his amusement and his love. So fierce was his passion that, like a true lover, he bemoaned even the few hours that he could not trade, and carried on a continuous struggle to lengthen the official time for dealing. Social life, dress, amusement, amours, these found no place at all in his desired life. Clever trades, new manipulations, big deals, these were the center of his existence.

Most of the other brokers were socially ambitious. They were good brokers and good livers. And they disliked Little; he did not conform, either in his general life

JACOB LITTLE

*The first of the manipulators. Four times his enemies
cornered him; three times he rallied, but the
fourth attack laid him low.*

or his trading approach. At first they laughed at him, then hated him, and when success followed success, began to fear him. Four times their combined attacks forced him into bankruptcy. Three times he reëstablished himself and returned to plague his associates, but the fourth attack laid him low.

Not having any precedent in manipulation to work by, his methods were all original. His schemes were uniformly successful, but a tendency to over-extend himself was later the cause of his downfall.

His coup in Erie served as a basis for one of Daniel Drew's major manipulations many years later. The panic of 1837 had been attended by the repudiation of various State bond issues. Many of these securities had been in currency in the London market, and the loss attendant to the repudiation of these issues had diverted the English investors' unfailing interest in the American market to the railroad securities. For some unfathomable reason, the paper of the Erie Railroad, issued in 1833, had from the beginning a peculiar fascination for the English. A large number of Erie bonds, convertible into stock, had been purchased there. Little started a bear campaign against Erie shares. His method was to sell large blocks of the stock on sellers' options ranging from six to twelve months. A clique of brokers, who long had been distressed at his unorthodox activities, decided to corner him and force him out of the market. When Little's contracts matured, his finish seemed imminent.

The price had been run up so high and the supply of stock had been so carefully gathered in, that it seemed impossible for the original bear to meet his obligations. This situation, coupled with the fact that the directors of the Erie were members of the clique opposed to Little, seemed to clinch the situation for the "Little Bear's" opponents. It seemed that they had him cornered at last, but they had not counted on Little's ingenuity. Some time before he had quietly sent over to London and purchased a large quantity of convertible bonds. These bonds he converted into stock and on the day of maturity, he triumphantly delivered the stock to his surprised opponents. The discovery of the possibility of using the convertible feature of railroad bonds in a market manipulation was later used with excellent effect by Drew, Gould and Fisk.

During these purely manipulative transactions, the regular business of the brokers again seriously declined. Business depression and a period of dullness in the trading market succeeded the panic of 1837, and by 1840, the public interest in trading had so fallen off that the Stock Exchange Board, discouraged by the lack of business, voted to divide its surplus of about $20,000 among its eighty-eight members. This resolution, fortunately, was not put into effect, and a subsequent revival before the actual liquidation could be effected, assured the continuation of the Exchange.

About 1836, a rival organization had been formed

to compete with the New York Stock and Exchange Board. In this outlaw exchange, called the Bourse, or New Board, the smaller speculators did their trading. An anonymous author of the time thus described the crowd who made this market their headquarters: "They have neither trade nor profession of any kind, and if they ever had any they have abandoned it. Some of them are of that class called gentlemen, who have married fortunes and squandered them; some are broken merchants; some disgraced politicians . . . and some of them are loafers. They have neither wit enough to continue nor credit enough to carry out a speculation, but when one is begun . . . they may be seen flocking in and out of the brokers' offices, examining the stock books, talking wisely of the nation's affairs. Like flies around a honey pot, each one is anxious for a sip, and, according to his slender means, pledges $100, more or less, and orders his broker to buy as many shares as he will upon this security. They thus materially aid the great speculators; but the result to themselves, generally, is that their families or friends suffer precisely the amount they have risked."

To the new Merchants' Exchange Building erected at Wall and William Streets, the old board moved its quarters in 1842. It leased "the large hall over the reading room," more substantial quarters than it had ever had before. The initiation fee had been raised to $400, and the salaries of the officers had been increased. In the same building the New Board, or Bourse, also met, having at that time twenty members. By 1848, however, this rival exchange went out of business, most of its members having been taken into the Stock and Exchange Board. Sessions had been advanced to start at 10:30 in the morning. They lasted from then until noon, and from 2:45 to 3 in the afternoon. At one end of the meeting room was the rostrum, at which the president stood to call the stocks. The secretary recorded all transactions. The members, picturesquely attired in the uniform dress of swallow-tail coats, high stocks and tall hats, had their seats around a long table and on two raised platforms. Brokerage was then a genteel business, and the members watched with no kindly reaction the rapid invasion of their exclusive province by a new type of broker, whose aggressiveness and ingenuity were superior to his social standing and taste in dress.

Meanwhile, as Daniel Drew put it, "railroads now were spreading over the country like measles in a boarding school." Government favor and free grants of land to the pioneer builders gave a fresh impetus to the development. The public began to take increasing interest in stocks, and the Stock Exchange a renewed lease on life. But no competitor to Little arose, and he alone it was who continued manipulative tactics. Not until after 1850, when first Drew and then Vanderbilt entered the Exchange arena, did any other great manipulative figure dominate the scene. In banking circles, August

THE FIRST MERCHANTS' EXCHANGE

Erected in 1826 on Wall Street near William Street, on the present site of the National City Bank.

THE MERCHANTS' ROOM OF THE EXCHANGE

As it looked in 1831.

Belmont, who came to New York from Havana to represent the Rothschilds when the Joseph Brothers went to the wall in the panic of 1837, was a respected leader. Among the operators, there were a few, like Henry Keep, whose taste for ostentatious display was probably nurtured by a boyhood spent in a poorhouse, who attempted comparatively large speculations. Keep and William Webb were bold and successful but their manipulations were in no way original. There was also William H. Marston, who one evening gave the most extravagant dinner New York had ever seen, and the next morning went broke for half a million. With the coming of Daniel Drew and Commodore Vanderbilt into the Street, however, the scope of market activities was to enter into so tremendous an extension that even to-day with our eight-million-share days, their ventures seem titanic. From the very first, both by temperament and interests, Daniel Drew and Vanderbilt found themselves opposed to each other in almost every major coup. Where Drew used cunning Vanderbilt used force. Drew was naturally a bear, a natural successor of Jacob Little. Vanderbilt was an incorrigible optimist, a bull leader and a remorseless fighter. They had fought each other in the old steamboat days before either had entered the railroad field and the exchange market. Their struggle was to be intensified with the extension of their interests and the widening scope of their transactions.

A panic first gave Jacob Little his chance, and a panic

caused his fourth and final downfall. In finance, as in politics, great names are made in revolution. When the machinery breaks down new mechanics get their chance. And when the country, intoxicated by a seeming new era of unprecedented prosperity, urged on by financiers and soothed by governmental ratification, went on a buying spree, the wise ones looked for a fall. Railroad builders were projecting more than they could accomplish, building more than they could pay for. The credit structure wobbled, tottered and finally crashed.

II

The process that led to the final disintegration was slowly gathering force as early as 1851 although the final débacle did not come until six years later. Once before, in 1837, our industrial structure had cracked under the strain of excessive currency inflation. Now a more complicated organization and a perfect fury of expansion made the disaster of 1857 the more dire in its effects.

The industrial and financial progress of the period between the two panics was not seasoned. Banks were easy to start; they had elastic currency-issuing privileges, they were very profitable, so why not start one? So thought many local financiers more dazzled by rapid enrichment than burdened by technical knowledge. In New York City alone twelve new banks were started in

1851 and fifteen more in the next two years. Formed mainly, or so it would seem from their activities, to take advantage of the liberal note-issuing privilege, these banks formed a vulnerable link in the country's financial chain.

This rapid development in financial accommodation seemed to most of the public warranted by conditions. Event after event added to the current optimism. As early as 1839, William F. Harnden started his personal express service, a venture which was to develop into a great business. Wells and Fargo were building up their delivery system between Chicago, Cincinnati and St. Louis. By 1844 the first telegraph line was built from Washington to Baltimore, and in the next year, New York and Philadelphia were connected. Railroads from everywhere to everywhere else, and from nowhere to nowhere, were rapidly projected, hastily built and slowly operated. To top it all, gold was discovered in California, some $50,000,000 of new metal was added to the country's resources and optimism knew no bounds.

A few keen eyes saw the cracks in the structure, and as always since, Wall Street's leaders waved the red light before the danger was apparent to the optimistic public. As early as January, 1857, before any evidence of coming disaster was visible to the untrained eye, Leonard W. Jerome, together with William R. Travers, engaged in a bear campaign on the theory of an inflated credit condition. They succeeded in starting a drop in security prices but industrial conditions seemed too promising to the public to cause public selling in any large quantity. Their premonition was soon justified. Unfortunately, Jerome and Travers were right.

On August 24, 1857, the Ohio Life Insurance and Trust Company, one of the most substantial and respected of the New York banks, was forced into bankruptcy by a sudden run and inability to realize quickly on its loans. The Ohio failed with liabilities of $5,000,-000, and started an overwhelming series of sympathetic failures. Other banks immediately began to call their loans as a precautionary measure, and this sudden contraction of credit, coming without notice, served the more to destroy confidence and make cumulative the force of the blow. On October 13th, eighteen banks in New York suspended specie payment, and this step was generally followed throughout the country. "The loafers in 10,000 bar rooms," said Horace Greeley, on October 15th, "who are to-day cursing the banks as broken, have themselves caused whatever there may be of bank insolvency by buying food and clothes for their families at the neighboring store and not paying for them when required." Put in these simple terms, the reason was correct. An unprecedented expansion of credit had taxed the elasticity of the machinery.

Prices on the Stock Exchange went down precipitously. In January, for example, Erie sold for $64 a share and New York Central at $95. By October of the same

year Erie was down to $18 and New York Central was
at $53. The irresponsible system of bank note issues,
especially those of the "wild-cat" institutions in the new
West, had paved the way for an unhealthy credit inflation. The ensuing and inevitable correction eventually
brought the financial system once more to a normal condition, although its suddenness and violence brought
with it a great deal of hardship to the country.

During this trying period, the existence of the organized Stock Exchange proved a stabilizing influence.
At such a time, when the public usually vents its fury
upon this central body, it most justifies its functions.
Although the securities listed on the board suffered
severe drops, the fall was minor compared with unlisted
securities dealt with directly. For such paper there was
no ready market, and those forced to sell could do so
only through sales at auction, and at sacrifices more
severe than similar stocks which had a ready, if a depre-
ciating, market on the Exchange Board.

It was soon realized that it is in a selling period that
the Exchange is most necessary, and many outside brokers tried to secure seats. As a result of the unusual number of applicants, the New York Stock Exchange in
May, 1858, increased its initiation fee to $1,000, al-
though for a broker's clerk of three years' standing only
$500 was required. Payment of the initiation fee was
not, however, the only requirement. Gradually, perhaps
because of their experience with Jacob Little, there had

grown up among the members a feeling that a certain
social station should be required of the applicants. There
was also a prejudice against the younger men and only
those who persisted and fought for entrance were able
to secure admission under any conditions. Thus Henry
Clews, then a rising young financier, says in his *Fifty
Years of Wall Street,* that "the old fellows were united
together in a mutual admiration league and fought the
young men tooth and nail, contesting every inch of
ground when the young men sought entrance to their
sacred circle." In a way, of course, the attitude of the
members of the inner circle could be understood. They
felt that they were the possessors of a valuable privilege
and the custom of selling seats on the Exchange had not
yet been thought of. Merely by payment of the initiation fee a young man could secure all the privileges of
a valuable attendance right, and this notion struck a
good many young men on the fringes of Wall Street at
the same time. The more aggressive of them succeeded,
either by diplomacy or by force, and in spite of the
difficulties and organized opposition in securing admit-
tance. Some of them had to resort to arbitrary tactics to
gain their places. Thus Henry Clews, after several unsuccessful attempts, inserted an advertisement in the
newspapers that he would buy and sell stocks at a
commission of a sixteenth of one per cent, as against the
regular Exchange rate of one-eighth. Clews diverted a
great deal of business from the regular channels and

was soon taken in by the Board as a measure of self-protection. As a clerk of standing he paid only the initiation fee of $500 for his seat, a privilege still retained by his firm and now worth more than half a million dollars.

The radical shaking up of the financial community incidental to the failure of 1857 gave many younger men a chance to come forward. When the Ohio Trust went down, Jacob Little was one of those who fell with it for the fourth and final blow. Strange enough, his failure was due to selling short. Although he had the right idea and would have made a huge fortune from these operations could he but have held on, Little had so overextended himself that a slight bulge before the final crash found him at the mercy of his opponents. He had sold more than 100,000 shares of Erie short, and was unable to carry his position. The first of the great manipulators failed for $10,000,000 on December 5, 1856, during a period of rising prices just before the great drop started. He went on the floor again a few months later. His credit weakened, his confidence shaken and his former confederates newly allianced, found him in a vulnerable position in August, 1857, when the upheaval started. His position was on the right side, but it took only a slight blow to force him from the field. On August 26th, he gave way as the leader to Daniel Drew who had crowded his way in among the leaders via the Erie road.

CHAPTER IV

DREW AND VANDERBILT

THE Wall Street of the '50's and early '60's was dominated by the alliances, friendships, struggles and coups of Daniel Drew and Cornelius Vanderbilt. Sometimes as allies, and sometimes as merciless opponents, these two were principals in almost every major operation. By nature they were exact opposites, but some mysterious personal attraction had made them close personal friends and business allies even before either of them had entered the Wall Street arena.

Drew, born in 1797, was three years younger than Vanderbilt. He had come into the steamboat business after Vanderbilt, but was soon the Commodore's most important competitor on the Hudson. As a boy his favorite motto was, "If a cat would eat fish she must be willing to wet her feet." His attitude in all his dealings was consistent with this policy. In his early life he had been in turn circus man, drover and innkeeper. As a circus man he got religion and to the end of his life this intense interest alternated with his absorption in the manipulations of Wall Street. His religious enthusiasms were so intense that his interest was almost morbid and

DANIEL DREW

"Daniel says, 'up!'; Erie goes up. Daniel says 'down!';
Erie goes down. Daniel says 'wiggle-waggle!';
it bobs both ways."

in its exercise he released what little of finer human feeling there was in his nature.

Daniel Drew had been a great success as a drover. His dealings in cattle had been very profitable and it was not long before he became the leader in that business in New York's butcher trade. Driving down the Harlem Valley one day with a herd of cattle he came upon an idea that helped to make him wealthy and added a racy expression to the Wall Street vocabulary. Henry Astor, John Jacob's brother, was one of the largest butchers in New York and an important customer for drovers. Drew had not been very successful in selling to him because Astor wanted fat cattle, and Daniel's cattle, like himself, were lank and lean, bought cheaply and starved. Crossing the Harlem at the King's Bridge, about where Third Avenue now crosses 125th Street, Daniel put up for the night. When all the cattle boys were asleep Drew went out to the drove in the pasture and emptied sacks of salt on the ground. By morning the cattle were choked for water. In the meantime word was sent to Henry Astor that Drew was on his way with some prime cattle and to meet him at noon. Not a drop of water did the cattle get till they reached the Bull's Head Tavern and shortly before Astor arrived. Then they were let loose; the salt had done its work, and they sucked up the water like sponges. By the time Astor came out to look, a plump lot of cattle was there to meet him. Astor tried to hide his enthusiasm, but Drew got three cents a pound for cattle that weighed up exceedingly well. Wall Street took the term "watered stock" from this drover's trick.

Drew's interest in steamboating dated from an investment of a thousand dollars he made at the earnest entreaty of a friend in a boat called the "Water Witch." This boat went on the Hudson in competition with the boats of Cornelius Vanderbilt and his brother Jake, but could not keep up with the Commodore's faster ships and lost money. Vanderbilt teased him about it and Drew resolved to go into the business on a larger scale and beat the Commodore at his own game. He raised capital for a new company, built faster ships, and soon had Vanderbilt suggesting an alliance. This was arranged. With the elimination of the competition, both of them did well thereafter and fattened their private fortunes for bigger game. In the meanwhile, the railroad had come in and promised larger opportunities. It was not long before both Vanderbilt and Drew were in the field and, characteristically, at the top of the heap.

About the same time, Drew, always with an eye to any center of activity, realized that Wall Street, with the extension of railroad enterprise, was becoming increasingly important. As owner of the Bull's Head Tavern, the drovers' trading center, he had gradually taken on some of the duties of a private banker for the drovers. He found that holding and using other people's money could be made profitable and the bank-

CORNELIUS VANDERBILT

"Put it up to a thousand!," ordered the Commodore,
"this panel game is being tried too often."
And the Harlem corner was on.

ing and brokerage firm of Drew, Robinson and Company was the result. "The best fishing is in deep waters," thought Daniel Drew, and right enough he was. From the very first "Uncle Daniel," as he was generally called, and none too affectionately, was singularly lacking in popularity on the Street. James Medberry, in his "Men and Mysteries of Wall Street," published in 1878, notes in speaking of Drew, that "the belief that he never hesitates to sacrifice his friends, if the necessities of speculation require it, is entertained with such unanimity in the money quarter, and is illustrated by so many anecdotes that one is compelled to acquiesce in it. The foible is the more salient on account of the genuine piety of the man. . . . He has built churches, founded a theological seminary, and given away prodigally to individual charities. Yet he has the reputation of being close in the extreme. Probably the secret of this amazing contradiction between facts and opinion is to be found in the enmities which his daring, subtle and obscure speculations have excited. He is the 'Sphinx of the Stock Market.' " Drew at first confined his financial activities to speculation and banking. He realized very soon, however, that the only way he could engineer manipulations was as an insider and by a careful campaign wormed his way into the directorate of the Erie Railroad. This was just before the beginning of the Civil War and it is at this point that Uncle Daniel comes into our story.

Although closely affiliated with Drew in many major operations Vanderbilt was an entirely different type of man. Just as Drew was by nature and temperament a bear, so was the Commodore by nature and preference a bull. Drew was secretive and suspicious; Vanderbilt was talkative and friendly. Hearty and buoyant, a lover of horses and of life, Vanderbilt fought openly if remorselessly. But the two men had one trait in common, a characteristic that was, and possibly still is, absolutely necessary to the retention of power in Wall Street. They knew how to glide over every moral restraint with almost childlike disregard. So necessary is this ability, that John D. Rockefeller, master of this negative virtue, has said that he was willing to pay a substitute a salary of a million dollars a year, if, besides other positive qualities, he had no scruples whatsoever and was ready to kill off thousands of victims without a murmur.

Vanderbilt found his work early in life. It was as a steamboat operator on Staten Island that he made his first financial venture and it was in this field that he found his early success. By 1845 he was already worth three-quarters of a million. With the discovery of gold in California, he extended the scope of his enterprises to meet the travel demand, and by dint of a fierce energy and brilliant judgment soon dominated that profitable field. His dominance was attained, however, not without steady competition and ceaseless struggle. In such an atmosphere he was very much at home, and the other men who tried to match him could do little against his driving attacks. His methods were always direct, often brutal, and uniformly successful. To some associates, who had taken advantage of his absence abroad to manipulate the stock of the Accessory Transit Company in which he was largely interested, he wrote:

Gentlemen:

You have undertaken to cheat me. I will not sue you because the law takes too long. I will ruin you.

Sincerely yours,
Cornelius Vanderbilt.

He set about this task systematically and within a year had the satisfaction of seeing his threat fulfilled.

His transcontinental steamship business necessitated the co-operation of Central American governments and he set out to form armies, foment rebellions and organize expeditions to assure the political background he required for his steamship ventures. From a small ferrying scheme he had by 1860 extended his interests to ocean shipping, and besides being the dominant figure in that business was probably the most powerful individual figure in American finance. At the beginning of the Civil War he was worth $15,000,000. Characteristic of the man is his abandonment of the steamship business entirely as soon as he had convinced himself that greater opportunities lay in railroading. He was seventy years old when he made this important change. With the advent of both Vanderbilt and Drew into this growing field, Wall Street was to see the entry of two titans who were to dominate the activities of Wall Street, startle the country with their unprecedented operations and lay the basis for some of the most striking manoeuvres in speculative history.

II

In 1862 Vanderbilt decided to purchase some stock in the Harlem Railroad. Twenty years before some friends had suggested that he go into the Harlem but he flatly refused to have anything to do with railroads. "I'm a steamboat man," he said, "a competitor of these steam contraptions that you tell us will run on dry land. Go ahead! I wish you well, but I never shall have anything to do with 'em." He had now changed his mind and was prepared to make a cautious entry. When he went into the Harlem it was selling at eight dollars a share. In the same year, under the impetus of his purchases, it rose as high as $30 a share, and by April, 1863, when his open market purchases had assured him control, it reached $50. The road ran through the Harlem Valley and terminated at Fourth Avenue and Twenty-sixth Street in New York. He realized that extension further downtown was important, and as soon as control was sure he induced the Common Council to extend his right of way down Broadway to the Battery. With characteristic energy, he immediately proceeded to dig up the street and lay rails to the new terminus. While Vanderbilt had been making his original purchases for control, Daniel Drew was also accumulating Harlem shares, although on a smaller scale. While not working directly with the Commodore, he had been apprised of his plans and had taken on a strong line of the stock. Boss Tweed had also accumulated a large amount of stock at Vanderbilt's suggestion and helped on the political end. The Commodore was content to make a legitimate profit on the rise in the stock attendant upon the extension of the road, and proceeded to extend the line further and build up its business. Drew's nature could not be satisfied with any such normal profit. He conceived the idea of getting together with Tweed—and instituting a bear campaign against Vanderbilt in Harlem, the idea being to have the aldermen repeal the Broadway franchise and thus force the stock down. Tweed was willing, and he and Drew proceeded to liquidate their holdings preparatory to putting into effect their campaign of depression. This was in May, and Harlem stock was selling at about $100 a share, its rise having been steady, both because of Vanderbilt's aggressive development of the road, and also because the success of the Union forces in the war had given the general market a boost. At the $100 figure, Drew and

Tweed disposed of their holdings, and then proceeded to sell the stock short in large volume. Some of the leaders of the aldermen and the Common Council had also been apprised of the plan, and formed a separate smaller syndicate to sell the stock. With the hearty co-operation of the aldermen, it did not seem the coup could fail. Soon afterward, Tweed gave the signal, and the Board and Common Council passed an ordinance reconsidering their former decision as to the Broadway franchise, and rescinding the grant. Tweed and the Council had taken Vanderbilt's bribes but then they had done what they had promised. They had passed the franchise, but nothing had been said about not repealing it. When the news came out, Harlem dropped precipitously to $72 a share, almost before Vanderbilt realized the turn events had taken. The shorts, however, did not yet cover. It looked certain that the stock would go to 50 and possibly lower. But the sturdy Commodore was not yet beaten. He decided to sustain the market and battle Drew, Tweed and the city government. He put a large share of his fortune behind his plan of support and bought every share of Harlem offered. His support made the market firm at 72. Below this point it would not budge. The shorts finally realized that something was wrong and prepared to cover and take their small profit. But Vanderbilt wasn't satisfied to let them get out so easily. There were 110,000 shares of Harlem outstanding and the shorts had sold 27,000 shares more than that num-

WALL STREET IN THE FORTIES

WALL STREET IN THE FIFTIES

ber. As soon as Vanderbilt saw that they were ready to cover, he jumped the price to 100, then to 150, to 170 and finally to 179. At that price he let the Common Council and their friends buy the stock and take their loss. The Commodore had already made a few millions from the attempt of Tweed and his crowd and felt he had got his bribes back with compound interest. Drew took his loss. However, the profits on his original purchases of Harlem had been so great that he was still ahead in Harlem. He was not yet ready to admit Vanderbilt could beat him, and tried a new variation of his original plan.

After the betrayal by the New York City Council, Vanderbilt determined to go to Albany and get his franchise directly from the State Legislature which was not under Tweed's influence. Knowing of these plans, Drew proceeded to buy the influence of most of the leaders, although fully aware that Vanderbilt had also paid them for their votes. Drew figured that they would be faithful to him, after their fashion, because they could make, besides the bribes, a neat profit on the turn in the stock. Entirely undaunted, Drew proposed to repeat the original Harlem bear transaction. After the settlement with the shorts, Harlem had receded to $75 a share. A favorable report, instigated by Drew, was given out from the Legislature in Albany as to the prospect for a Broadway franchise for the Harlem. The stock jumped from $75 to $150 a share in a few days, and Drew proceeded to sell short. The chief members of the Legislature also went short and with them all their friends. As soon as they had sold all they could at the top price of $150 a share, they proceeded to take up the petition for the franchise and defeated the bill by an overwhelming vote. Since Vanderbilt now had no other legislative body he could turn to, they figured that the decline of the stock would be rapid. It was for a time. In two days the price fell fifty points. But suddenly and unaccountably a new rise in Harlem began. The stock was quoted at 110; it went up to 127; to 140; to 150; then to 185. Also, strangely enough, not once had the Commodore come to Albany or sent a representative to sue for terms. The members of the Legislature were in this operation very deeply—in fact, too deeply to avert ruin. Many of them had conducted their operations on borrowed money, and almost all of them had sold all the stock they possibly could. A few of the more timid ones covered and more tried to follow. But by that time stock was not obtainable at any price. Once again, more stock had been sold for future delivery than was actually in existence. And this time Vanderbilt had made up his mind that his opponents would pay and pay mightily. He was most angry at Drew, whose tricks he had so many times forgiven. A few days more and the price was up to 285. "Put it up to a thousand," ordered the Commodore, "this panel game is being tried too often." Leonard Jerome and John Tobin were in with

Vanderbilt. They pointed out that it might be better not to press the shorts too hard, and $285 was the figure finally set at which Vanderbilt would be generous enough to let his opponents have their stock for settlement. At that figure most of the members of the Legislature meekly settled. Drew threatened litigation, delayed settlement, alternately fought and pleaded with Vanderbilt, and finally cajoled him into letting him make a private compromise settlement. Drew gave Vanderbilt a check for half a million and was released from his contract to deliver. Both the loss in money and in prestige hit Drew hard. It soon got to be a saying in the Street in designating any kind of a hard knock: "He went short of Harlem." This time Drew felt, not for the last time, the force of his little jingle:

He that sells what isn't his'n,
Must buy it back or go to prison.

III

Running in competition with the Harlem road was the New York and Hudson River Railroad, known in the Street as the Hudson. Vanderbilt decided he could increase the profits of both of these roads by a consolidation, and proceeded to buy up the stock of the Hudson on the open market preparatory to putting his plan into effect. By the early part of 1864, he had succeeded in buying control at an average price of $25 a share, and went to Albany to get permission for the consolidation of the roads. The members of the Legislature, many of whom had been hurt badly in the Harlem corner, accepted his bribes but were not disposed to give the Commodore any favorable action. In fact an abortive attempt was made to repeat the Harlem short campaign, but this move was quickly squelched by Vanderbilt. Permission for consolidation was not forthcoming, however, and the roads were operated separately although functioning as a unit wherever possible. The acquisition of the Hudson only whetted the appetite of the Commodore and he set out to secure control of still another road, the New York Central. This road ran from Albany to Buffalo and its acquisition would give Vanderbilt a continuous railway line from New York City to the Great Lakes. His attempt was inaugurated in 1864, but so determined was the opposition of the owners, that it was not until November, 1867, that he finally succeeded in securing control. To do this, he had had to buy $18,000,000 worth of New York Central stock on the open market. By the fall of 1869, the Legislature had changed its complexion sufficiently to enable Vanderbilt to push through his consolidation plans. In that year he secured the passage of an act permitting him to unite the Harlem, the Hudson and the New York Central into one road, and the stock of each of these roads reflected the consolidation by an immediate jump. The capital of the constituent roads was increased from $44,000,000 to $86,000,000, and Vanderbilt voted himself $6,000,000 in cash and $20,000,000 in new stock as a bonus for his efforts. This combination thus effected made Vanderbilt the most important single factor in eastern transportation, and now only the Erie Railroad, controlled by Daniel Drew and his crowd, had escaped his grasp. This road was a valuable piece of property, although its present management was not conducive to a profitable operation. The Erie was used by Drew and his associates mainly for manipulative operations, but it might at any time, under fair management, turn into a dangerous rival to Vanderbilt's roads. Realizing this, Vanderbilt decided to force his way in and, if possible, secure control of the Erie and complete his monopoly of eastern traffic. This program was not to be as easily carried out as his previous efforts, for a new figure had come up in Wall Street and allied himself with Drew. A young broker by the name of Jay Gould had been finding his place among the Wall Street giants and was to give the seventy-five year old Commodore the first beating of his long career.

CHAPTER V

JAY GOULD

JAY GOULD was born at Roxbury, New York, on May 27, 1836, of Scottish and Puritan stock. There is no certain evidence of Jewish blood in the family, although the fact that the original name of the family was Gold has led some writers to make that assumption. Thus Henry Adams called Gould "the complex Jew." His father was a poor farmer, and the boy's childhood was difficult and trying. His schooling was limited and fragmentary, in spite of the fact that it was Jay's one boyhood ambition to be thoroughly educated. Even in his teens, he expressed an ambition to go into railroading, an ambition which was to be thoroughly fulfilled. Thus his elder sister writes of him: "He did not engage very much in sports; he did not have much time. In the winter he would sometimes ride down on a sled, perhaps once or twice, but he really didn't have any time for sports, because he was always either studying or reading. He never played baseball, checkers, or cards. When he was twelve or thirteen years old, he was studying geometry and logarithms and getting ready for surveying. He was thinking about build-

[100]

ing a railroad across the Continent, so that California might be nearer to us."

A busy, a hard but not a happy childhood! His schooling over, still a boy, he went out to make his way among men. In the light of his later life, the title of Jay's last school composition is interesting. It was headed, "Honesty is the Best Policy."

As a youth of seventeen, he wrote to a friend, "I think I shall realize enough to see me through Yale College, and that is the extent of my hopes. Perhaps it is an idle dream but a vision of imagination. I say there is no room for idle speculations when they conflict with a deep resolution to accomplish worthy ends, and I hope that a kind Providence that has thus far sheltered me under her wing will crown my at least honest exertions with a sphere of usefulness."

Jay Gould's analysis of the purpose of an education was not the common one. It was not a thirst for learning, a desire to understand and an urge to develop the mind. Jay conceived of an education as a means of placing one "where he is capable of speaking and acting for himself without being bargained away and deceived by his more enlightened brothers," and "as a means of controlling the human destiny in yielding happiness and enjoyment to its possessor." There is a clear indication of the development of a powerful defensive mechanism, the natural urge of the weak and the embittered to strike before the stronger can crush. The clear, precocious mind of the boy was being sharpened for action.

In the adolescent period of Jay Gould's life we still see symptoms of a changing mind and a varying mood. His temperament was forming and his character hardening. After that, there was a firm consistency—the storming for power, the mental ruthlessness, the singleness of purpose, and the genius of the great buccaneer. Jay Gould, at sixteen, frail, sentimental, superintelligent, precocious, an expiring piousness still in his system, affectionate, a born trader and a ruthless fighter, starts out to conquer the world. Disappointed in his dreams of securing a proper education, he turns his thoughts to the struggle for wealth. An inferiority complex, hardship, social isolation, the uncouthness of his people, and the knowledge of his family's fall from prestige to a bitter struggle for survival, have developed in the boy a compensating defense mechanism, and sharpened his ambition to acquire wealth and power. From that time on he was against the world and the world was against him.

An industrial nation is being born. The 1850's, the era of railroads and industry, the beginning of big business—the stage is set for manipulation and corruption. In Wall Street Daniel Drew, Cornelius Vanderbilt and Jacob Little are already on the scene. In upstate New York, Jay Gould is planning a venture in surveying, the first venture on his own account. At seventeen he is already to sense the possibility of using others for one's

JAY GOULD

Vanderbilt called him the smartest man in America.

own advancement. His methods are from the beginning
the methods of Jay Gould, speculator and financier—
to use the other fellow, but to make it worth his while
to be used; to give only to those from whom one can
receive; to give in order to get—and to get much more
than you give.

Jay Gould found his way to Wall Street in 1861 at
the age of twenty-five, after a varied career in surveying and map-making, a venture in authorship and a
partnership in a leather business. In this business, he
had been successful and had built up a large tannery in
Pennsylvania. Charges of fraud were, however, made
by his partner, who had originally furnished all the
capital, and after a hectic struggle, Gould was forced
out and came to New York almost penniless. His marriage to the daughter of a wealthy grocer, Philip Miller,
gave him the chance for a new start. His father-in-law
had a long time before made what turned out to be an
unfortunate investment in a sixty-two mile railroad
running from Troy, New York, to Rutland, Vermont.
This neglected road, called the Rutland and Washington, was in its last stages of decay. The stock of the
road was worth nothing on the market, and the first
mortgage bonds were selling at ten cents on the dollar.
Miller sent Jay up to look things over, more to give his
son-in-law something to occupy him, rather than in
hope of retrieving anything from the investment. Jay
was familiar with the territory; he had been reared in

the vicinity and as a surveyor had covered a large part of the ground. After several weeks spent in going over the road, Gould reported back to Miller that the trunk road had possibilities under proper management and asked his father-in-law to lend him enough money to purchase control. Eager to give Jay a start Miller consented, and Gould at twenty-four became President, Treasurer and Superintendent of the Rutland line. His idea was to build up the little road and then attempt to sell it to one of the numerous railroad consolidations then being formed. His management of the road must have been excellent, for within a few months the managers of the Rensselaer and Saratoga Railroad combination purchased Gould's road for $130,000, the larger part of which was profit.

Jay had started out in the railroad field with a bang, and from that day to the end of his life considered himself a railroad man. We do not have many details of Gould's first coups. He was still working entirely alone and not on large roads. He saw great possibilities in this field of buying up small trunk roads and selling them to large consolidations.

Another opportunity came to him in the same year. In 1860 a friend told Gould that he had bought control of the Cleveland and Pittsburgh Railroad. Gould's friend had over-extended himself and could not meet his notes. The stock had been purchased by him at $60 a share but, in view of his financial difficulties, he was willing to sell at a much lower figure. Jay made a quick investigation and, using the profits from the Rutland sale, bought fifty-one per cent of the stock of the road from his friend at $40 a share. The line soon began to pay dividends, but Jay, instead of trying to build it up as a permanent business, began to look around for a purchaser. Fortunately the Pennsylvania Railroad needed the Cleveland and Pittsburgh to complete its system; in fact, needed it badly enough to buy Jay out at $120 a share.

Gould felt that he had finally found his life work. He liked railroads. His first successful attempt with the Rutland had given him confidence and a comparatively large capital. Within a year he had been able to net a profit of more than $100,000. For dealing on a large scale the best place was Wall Street, and so, in 1861, the newly painted sign of SMITH, GOULD AND MARTIN, BROKERS, announced that Jay Gould, then just turned twenty-five, had come to join the speculative fraternity.

Jay Gould had all the gambler's qualities without the gambler's two great faults—generosity and pity. There is no mart where the perfect gambler's expertness is better tested than in Wall Street, and there have been few times when for its successful practice such expertness was more necessary than in 1861. As Daniel Drew put it, "Along with ordinary happenings, we fellows in Wall Street now had, in addition, the fortunes of war to speculate about, and that always makes great doings on a stock exchange. It's good fishing in troubled waters."

Gould did not join in the war enthusiasm, nor help the Union cause in any way. He was not unpatriotic, but neither was he a rabid patriot. The Civil War was a great chance, and he set himself to the task of making money out of it. He was not yet one of the insiders. He had secured a certain standing in the Street as a clever trader but was making money in small parcels. A trade, a pool operation, or a manipulation of stocks on the basis of purchased advance information on the outcome of a battle were the extent of his wartime activities. His partners in Wall Street, Henry Smith and H. H. Martin, were active figures, but not of sufficient caliber or prestige to command valuable inside information or control. Gould slowly drew away from them and near the end of the Civil War was already making connections with the bigger men in the Street, such as Daniel Drew. The firm name of Smith, Gould & Martin continued for a long time, but it was merely a nominal partnership. Gould's outside interests became more extensive with time until finally the partnership was dissolved. The fate of his first associates in Wall Street was the fate of all who came too close to Gould and did not watch closely enough. Martin died bankrupt in an insane asylum, Gould's sworn enemy, and Smith was later broken and forced from the Street after a campaign against his former partner.

CHAPTER VI

THE ERIE RAIDS

THE ten years from 1860 to 1870 were to witness some of the most daring and spectacular financial freebooting ever attempted before that time or since. Most of the dramatic stock operations of the period were centered around the Erie Railroad, which although comparatively unimportant in itself, assumed a reflected importance through its being honored and looted by the great financial generals of the time. In these raids, which later turned into fierce struggles, Vanderbilt was aligned against the trickiest triumvirate of the time, Daniel Drew, Jay Gould and Jim Fisk.

The first three of the chief actors we have met before. To this formidable list, the name of James Fisk jr. must be added. Fisk had started life as a pedlar in Vermont. A natural salesman, he had prospered, and had become a traveler for the dry goods house of Jordan, Marsh and Company in Boston. The Civil War found him in Washington trying to sell blankets to the War Department. He was armed with letters to men of influence and some none too respectable women acquaintances in Washington. The combination was effective in enabling him to close some large contracts, and he took the precaution of making these contracts in his own name. As a consideration for turning them over, he was given a partnership in the firm. In Fisk's own words: "Our partnership didn't turn out very scrumptious. Those Boston merchants are so all-fired respectable! They are too conservative. They think the good name of the house with smaller profit is worth more than a smaller name with bigger profit. We didn't hit it off well together, and the upshot was they very soon asked me to leave. I did—for a consideration. They paid me $60,000 to get out. I started in the dry goods business myself; but it didn't go. Came to New York with what money I had left. I started in as a Wall Street operator. Result, lost every cent I had."

A year after this event, he presented himself at Daniel Drew's office with a proposition to sell for him some Stonington Railroad shares Drew owned, at an unusually high price. Drew was skeptical but let Fisk have a try at it, and to Drew's surprise, he was immediately successful in disposing of the shares to some Boston merchants. This impressed Drew who gave him some other jobs, all of which he handled to Drew's entire satisfaction and profit. After that he became Uncle Daniel's chief assistant in several ventures, and his unusual ability in negotiations made him a valuable henchman. They never trusted each other, but such a state was normal in the Street at the time, and was not permitted to

JAMES FISK, JR.

"Cheer up, my hearty! Nothing is lost save honor," was his
comment after the gold conspiracy collapsed.

interfere with their profitable operations. That this distrust was not without basis we can judge from the fact that it was Fisk who later was to ruin his benefactor and force him into bankruptcy.

The Erie Railroad was organized in 1833, but financial difficulties had prevented its completion until 1851. Its early operation was not successful, and in 1859 it passed into the hands of a receiver. The road might probably have been abandoned by its American originators had not English investors come forward with help. For some reason Erie always had a curious fascination for British investors, and through all its troublous times, a large British interest stood by and helped to pull it through its difficulties. During one of its recurrent periods of stress Daniel Drew had managed to force himself in as a member of the Board of Directors. By spreading rumors in the Street of the road's difficulties he had succeeded in bringing Erie stock down from $63 to $33 a share. Drew then offered to lend the road $1,500,000 on condition that he be made a director. The road needed money badly, and with its credit so weakened by the drop in its stock the management was glad to get this help. Then operating from the inside he forced the stock up and down almost at will, and it soon got to be a saying in the Street, "Daniel says 'Up!'; Erie goes up. Daniel says 'Down!'; Erie goes down. Daniel says 'Wiggle-waggle!'; it bobs both ways!"

By 1868, the Erie had expanded to 773 miles of track

and its reserve was something over $16,000,000. It was a valuable and profitable property, in spite of Drew's football tactics. The road was paying dividends, but Drew was making more on the Erie from his Wall Street operations than the road on its legitimate operation. He was regularly devoting a proportion of his profit to religious activities, but in spite of the split he was already a millionaire. At the height of his power, Drew took Jim Fisk and Jay Gould into the management of the Erie. It was not long afterward that the Erie became known among the brokers as "The Scarlet Woman of Wall Street."

For a long time Daniel Drew had been having his own way with the Erie. For the last five years he had been the ruling spirit in the road and the uncontested manipulator of its Stock Exchange fortunes. His success was beginning to attract other financiers to the Erie, the most formidable of whom was Cornelius Vanderbilt, Drew's Wall Street enemy. Along about 1866, Vanderbilt had publicly announced that he would get control of the road and throw Drew's crowd out. He said that Drew and his associates were nothing but common gamblers, and that he would see to it that Erie was put into safe hands. And Cornelius set out to make a thorough job of it.

In the meantime, Jay Gould had been worming his way into the inner circle. As a broker he had specialized in Erie, and through his customers controlled a large block of stock. He was slated for election to the Board of Directors. Drew, lining up his forces for the coming fight with Vanderbilt, needed all the help he could muster. He took Jay in as a member of the board, and they allied their forces. By the end of 1866, Drew, Fisk and Gould were organizing to meet Vanderbilt's attack on the fruitful Erie. The stage was set for one of the most bitter and amazing financial struggles in Wall Street history.

II

Vanderbilt instituted an open campaign to wrest control of the Erie Road and to force Drew and his gang out of the management. Drew had good reason to fear Vanderbilt, and after his several set-backs in previous skirmishes, was not disposed to underestimate the opposition. With Gould and Fisk planning with him, however, he felt safer, though none too confident. An advantage in Drew's favor was that he was holding the fort and could use the resources of the road itself to defend himself. Vanderbilt was confident, but not cocksure. He realized that he had a slippery crowd to deal with, and arranged to take in as allies a group of Boston capitalists, who had some years before purchased a large block of Erie as a preliminary to forcing a consolidation with a small road they owned, which ran from Boston to the Erie terminus at Newburgh. In return for the help of the Boston group, Vanderbilt, as soon as he had control, was to see that the Erie guaranteed the interest on the other road's bonds.

Drew, characteristically, approached Vanderbilt and suggested an alliance. But a succession of betrayals had hardened the Commodore and he refused any compromise. "Buy Erie," Vanderbilt told his brokers. "Buy it at the lowest figure you can, but buy it." The ruthless, merciless energy of the seventy-four-year-old Caesar of the railroads was set to override all obstacles. Those who stood in his way he was ready to annihilate.

To-day the Stock Exchange stands in the role of parent referee to the men who choose this merciless arena for the exercise of their acquisitive activities. Just as now the boxing referee calmly enforces the polite rules of the man-killing sport, so do the Marquis of Queensberry rules lend the aroma of respectability to the tactics of the Wall Street fraternity. In 1868 bare knuckles were more the way of the Exchange, and Vanderbilt, Drew, Gould and the rest recognized few of the present-day rules. Judges, legislatures, officials, even governments, were legitimate allies. Bribery, perjury and forgery were not uncommon tools. And yet the men, in private life, were by no means rogues. Vanderbilt did not feel his Wall Street life inconsistent with his firm ideas of fair play and sportsmanship; Drew did not think that religious endeavor precluded his right to legitimate stealing; nor did Gould feel that a ruthlessness below Canal Street was unbecoming in a man exceptionally gentle and kind in his family life. It was the game, and there never was a time when the game was more merciless or cruel.

The election for the new Board of Directors of the Erie Railroad was scheduled for March, 1868. Proxies were, as always, for sale. The Commodore's natural arrogance had been intensified by his long succession of victories, and the opposition of the triumvirate roused in him a potent wrath. To buy control of the Erie meant buying up its stock, which was almost all in the Street. It was a tremendous task and required millions. Besides, it was necessary to buy control in the face of the organized resistance of the men actually in control. Vanderbilt was not daunted. He proceeded to corner Erie stock. He saw no reason why he could not repeat his Harlem and Hudson performances.

On February 17th, Vanderbilt started the legal side of the battle by obtaining an injunction against the directors of the Erie restraining them from the payment of interest or principal of $3,500,000 borrowed from Treasurer Drew in 1866. This injunction was granted by Judge Barnard of the Supreme Court of New York. Two days later, Vanderbilt's attorney appeared again before the reliable Judge Barnard, whose co-operation had been purchased for the occasion, and petitioned for the removal of Drew from office. Barnard complied by temporarily suspending Drew as an officer and director, pending a hearing. Several other injunctions and writs were obtained, one of them requiring Drew to return to the Erie 68,000 shares of Erie stock alleged to have been illegally issued in 1866.

To these numerous court orders the Drew party paid no attention. Denouncing Barnard as a Vanderbilt tool, Drew proceeded to Binghamton, where Drew's favorite Supreme Court wearer of the ermine, Judge Balcom, held court. Under a judicial system permitting thirty-three judges of equal authority to entertain original actions all over the State, it was not difficult to obtain a conflicting order. Judge Balcom issued numerous injunctions against Vanderbilt and his party, as inclusive as were Judge Barnard's. Into the details of these orders we will not enter. Vanderbilt paid no more attention to Judge Balcom's rulings than did Drew to Judge Barnard's. Vanderbilt went on purchasing all the Erie stock he could get and Drew went on selling it to him. The strange writs and meaningless injunctions were meant for the public. The business of appealing to the law was, in effect, a play to the gallery. The real business at hand was handled regardless of the judicial edicts. The injunctions became so plentiful at one time that the Drew party found itself completely enjoined—on the one hand by an injunction forbidding them to move and on the other by a mandatory injunction (a recent legal invention) ordering them to act. What they were to do or not to do was not very clear to anybody,

CURBSTONE BROKERS IN 1864

When they congregated on William Street near Beaver, before they moved to Broad Street, their open air headquarters until 1921.

but it seemed like a good moment to start the shooting.

While the Commodore was pouring millions into the purchase of Erie stock Drew's party was selling. The smaller Wall Street men, remembering the Harlem and Hudson corners, wondered how Drew would come out. Drew, Gould and Fisk had apparently sold more Erie stock than was in existence. Vanderbilt had bought up every share on the market, and it began to look as if Drew and his young men were in for a tight squeeze; but this battle was not to be a repetition of the Harlem corners. The smart youngsters and the wily parson had the ace of trumps in their sleeve.

At the beginning of the battle Drew had prepared for this moment. At one of the earlier meetings of the Erie board, there had been voted an issue of ten million dollars of bonds convertible into stock, the proceeds of which were supposed to go into replacing the iron rails of the Erie with steel. The Executive Committee, controlled by Drew, had voted to sell the entire amount of these bonds at not less than 72½. It was on the basis of this issue that Drew had dared to sell thousands of shares he did not own. Within ten minutes after the committee had adjourned, five million dollars of convertible bonds were placed on the market, and by means of a wash transaction, Daniel Drew's broker was the purchaser of the entire amount. Immediately the bonds were converted into common stock, and fifty thousand shares of stock were at Drew's disposal. These were distributed to his several brokers for sale to the Commodore. Within three days, the other fifty thousand shares were also on the market, and Erie stock became as plentiful as injunctions, but not quite so cheap. Vanderbilt dug in and bought, bought, bought. On the 10th of March, 1868, Erie opened at $80 a share and, on Vanderbilt's purchases, rose to $83; suddenly fifty thousand shares came on the market all in a lump and Erie broke to seventy-one. Vanderbilt bought, more and more. When the gong sounded, Erie stood at $78 a share. By the close of the day, Vanderbilt had a new lot of one hundred thousand shares of Erie, and Drew and his party had more than seven million dollars of the Commodore's money. The printing press had stopped Vanderbilt.

"Well," chuckled Jim Fisk, "that injunction of the Commodore's was aimed at the freedom of the press. As freeborn Americans, we couldn't stand for that. Give us enough rag paper, and we'll hammer the everlasting tar out of that mariner from Staten Island." Vanderbilt was reeling from the shock of the unexpected attack. We will let Daniel Drew give his account of that exciting day:

"The president of the board called out the shares of the various railroads in usual order: 'Union Pacific! Wabash! New York Central!'—he met with a dead silence. Then he called out 'Erie!' Things broke loose at once. One of our brokers jumped out on the floor and offered a block of one thousand shares; he followed this up with another thousand; that with another, until he had offered five thousand shares of Erie—wanted to sell them right then and there. Vanderbilt's brokers took the first two or three thousand blocks cheerfully; but it was noticed that they looked surprised. Then, almost before our first broker had gone through, another sprang forward and offered blocks of Erie for sale, ten thousand in all. Our first broker followed up with five thousand more (that made up his ten thousand). Still another came and helped push along the landslide. He yelled out, 'A thousand shares of Erie for sale! A thousand more of Erie! Five thousand shares of Erie!' And so on, until his ten thousand shares were offered.

"By this time the Vanderbilt brokers were scared out of their wits. They got into communication with their master. They sent the message, 'Hell has broke loose!' to him. 'Thirty thousand shares of Erie have come down raining on us in the last half hour, with more coming out every minute. What shall we do?' All the answer he gave was, 'Support the market.' As he didn't seem at all flustered, his brokers got courage and took our offerings. They succeeded in absorbing the whole fifty thousand shares without letting the market sag more than a point or two.

"But now came the death stroke. These deliveries of stock were made right away. As soon as the Exchange saw that these certificates were crisp and new, with the printer's ink hardly dry on them, the secret was out. In defiance of Vanderbilt's injunction we had set our printing press to work.

"The landslide broke loose; for if we had been able to cut the legal red tape with which Vanderbilt had tried to tie our hands, had found a way to start the printing press to work once more—why, it was good night to the Commodore, because there is no limit to the blank shares a printing press can turn out. White paper is cheap—it is bought by the ream; printer's ink is also dirt cheap; and if we could keep on working that kind of deal—make Vanderbilt pay us fifty or sixty dollars for little pieces of paper that hadn't cost us two cents, we would very soon have all of his cash.

"It was, I guess, the darkest hour in Vanderbilt's life. He had staked his reputation and a good share of his fortune on this Erie fight; and now we had suddenly unmasked a battery that was pouring hot shot into his ranks thick and fast. No wonder his followers began to desert him. There was a small-sized panic all through the Vanderbilt party. Until now they had looked upon their leader as able to take care of them. Some had begun to think that he was a sort of supernatural person, but now he was no longer the high and mighty one.

"This was the moment we had been waiting for. In war it is good generalship to know when to strike. We now dumped the other fifty thousand shares on to the floor of the Exchange all to once. The price, which had been at eighty-three, dropped like a dead heifer. It was as though the bottom had fallen out. Down and down and down it went, clear to seventy-one. Considering the number of shares involved, and the size of the transaction, it was the biggest stroke Wall Street had ever seen. The Commodore himself wasn't able to stand out any longer. The price rallied a little before the day was over, for it was seen that he wasn't as yet entirely swamped; he took all the stock that was offered, even the last fifty thousand, and paid over his good cash for it. But the market had made a fatal break. Nothing he or his friends could do would bring it back again, and the day closed with me and my crowd gloriously on top."

Vanderbilt was in the tightest position of his stormy career. He had more than a hundred thousand shares of Erie nobody would buy and which he dared not sell. He had put into the struggle almost every available dollar. With opponents as unscrupulous as they were resourceful, he could not estimate what further load he might be called upon to carry. He talked horse and played whist with his usual confidence. He tried to mask his concern by deviating in no way from his usual routine, but there was no question that he was seriously worried.

It was on March 10th that Drew, Gould and Fisk had raked in Vanderbilt's seven million. On the morning of the 11th, the tricky triumvirate met in the Erie Railroad office to count their profits. Of the money they had raked in from Vanderbilt four million was in greenbacks and they set to tying the money into bundles. It was a happy party until a messenger came to inform them processes for contempt of court were being issued and Ludlow Street jail was in sight. Vanderbilt was on the trail, vowing to clap them all into jail before the sun went down that night. It was a foggy day. "There is no sun to go down, anyhow," said Jimmy. "For heaven's sake, shut up!" said Jay. "It looks as though we woke up the wrong passenger," said Daniel. "We have got to do something and do it almighty quick."

"I'll tell you what I am going to do," said Jimmy. "I'm going to get my share of this swag over to Jersey in about two jerks of a lamb's tail; also I'm going to live there myself for a while. Up in Brattleboro in my kid days, I used to see people avoid interviews with the sheriff by crossing the bridge over the Connecticut, and once there, they would let the Vermont sheriff whistle for them. I always did like the air of Jersey, and I've been working pretty hard, anyway. A little rest would do me good."

"Agreed," said Daniel and Jay, and the three started off on a very strange pilgrimage. With pockets crammed with securities and account books under their arms, the dignified Executive Committee of the Erie Railroad rushed off in the direction of the Jersey ferry. In a hackney coach accompanying them was four million dollars' worth of greenbacks. Jim Fisk liked to refer to them as the Commodore's "birthday cards." By ten o'clock the Executive Committee of the Erie was safely on the Jersey shore, out of the grasp of Vanderbilt's judges. Safely settled in Taylor's Hotel, the trio made plans to stay on the Jersey side for a while until the affair would blow over or Vanderbilt sue for terms. Rumors came across the river that Vanderbilt, desperate and violently angry, was sending fifty men over to kidnap the triumvirate and get them back into the jurisdiction of his New York judges.

Taylor's Hotel in Jersey City became Fort Taylor. Daniel Drew called in Chief of Police Fowler, and organized fifteen police as an armed guard. Inspector Masterson of the Erie Railroad supplied a force of railway detectives to patrol the wharves and the streets around the hotel. Three twelve-pound cannon were mounted on the piers, with the Hudson County Artillery in reserve. Jim Fisk became the "Admiral." Four lifeboats, manned by a dozen men each, armed with Springfield rifles, were put under his charge to guard the waterfront. Jay Gould operated the railroad from Jersey City, and had all the division heads report to him at Taylor's Hotel. Steps were taken to incorporate the Erie Railroad as a Jersey corporation, and notice was served on Vanderbilt that the fight was to a finish. Gould also announced that the passenger rate from New York to Buffalo would be reduced from seven dollars to five. This was an attempt to embarrass Vanderbilt's New York Central road, force a drop in its stock, and thus add to the complications of Vanderbilt's position. Nothing was left undone to harass and frighten Vanderbilt into some sort of a compromise. A bill was introduced in the New York Legislature legalizing the issue of stock brought out with the aid of the friendly printing press. Jay Gould made a secret trip to Albany in an effort, aided by a little persuasion and a lot of cash, to push the bill through.

Vanderbilt was having a pretty hard time of it. It was a slippery crowd he had to deal with, and, while his resources were large, they were tried to the limit, and his depleted supply of cash gave him little margin for safety. He was trying to support his stocks, keep judges and legislators happy with bribes, and keep up the spirit in his own camp. It took enormous amounts of ready cash, of which he had none too much at the time, and a great deal of nerve. The banks would not lend him money on the enormous amounts of Erie stock he had been forced to absorb; it was only by threatening further to depress New York Central stock, of which several banks held large amounts, that he could get any substantial credit accommodation. Vanderbilt was up against it and about ready to compromise.

The Commodore managed, by careful manoeuvring, to get a note to Drew which Fisk and Gould would not see. It was short and to the point.

> Drew: I'm sick of the whole damned business. Come and see me.
>
> > Vanderbilt.

The Commodore explained his offer of peace. "This Erie war has taught me that it never pays to kick a skunk." He found that he had enough money to buy up the Erie, but not enough to stop a two-by-four printing press. Drew was also getting tired of the tricky business. He missed his family, and his Jersey residence had put him out of touch with his numerous religious activities. The peace note was very welcome to him, and he decided to evade his partners and go over on Sunday, when no summons could be served on him. His intention was undoubtedly to make a peace with Vanderbilt favorable to himself, and let the others take care of themselves.

Gould and Fisk were not so easily tricked, however, and made it their business to follow Drew and attend the conference. At the first meeting nothing was accomplished except the preliminary overtures. Drew was cordial but Vanderbilt was curt. "Now, see here," he said in reply to Drew's pious reference to the old steamboat days and their good friendship, "let's not get gushy. Of course, I'd like to get affectionate and chat with you about old times; no one knows how my bowels yearn after you, Drew; but, as I understand it, this is a business interview. So, if you'll draw up to that table, and wipe the tobacco juice off your chin, we'll talk."

Battles on Wall Street are violent, but short. Tried friends of one day will be unremitting enemies the next and fellow conspirators the day after. Grudges remain, but hostilities cannot often be too long maintained. When money is involved, convenience will conquer dislike and expedience overcome anger. Vanderbilt could not have maintained his strained position much longer whatever his boast; at the same time, his opponents could not live forever in Jersey City. Drew missed his church, Jay Gould longed for his family, and Jim Fisk felt lonesome away from his ballet dancers. All in all, both camps were ready for peace. Vanderbilt was too powerful for the trio, and they were too clever for Vanderbilt.

The Commodore was willing to agree to peace, but not to a loser's terms. He demanded that all Erie stock he had been saddled with be bought back at what it cost him. Where the money was to come from, Vanderbilt neither knew nor cared. The only place it could come from, of course, was the reliable if rather anemic Erie treasury, for neither Drew, Gould nor Fisk were disposed to part with their profits.

In the peace negotiations, relations between Drew on the one side and Gould and Fisk on the other had become strained. Gould and Fisk never fully trusted Drew, but he was a powerful factor in the Street, and their leader, and they worked with him. But recently there had been strong evidence that Drew had set out to betray the others to Vanderbilt in exchange for good terms for himself, and they decided to go after him. Gould refused at first to agree to Vanderbilt's proposal, which Drew favored. After a whispered conference with Fisk, Jay spoke up. From this moment, he became the leader rather than the follower.

"Mr. Vanderbilt," he said, "we are willing to come to some arrangement. We will allow Drew here to keep the profits he has made in this deal, and to draw the money out of the Erie treasury. But there has got to be one condition attached; he has to get out of the Erie for good and all." Vanderbilt didn't care much what happened to the Erie—he was cured of any desire to get it over the very effective defensive methods of Gould

THE COMMODORE ON THE AVENUE

and Fisk—but he suggested putting the matter to a vote. Of course, everybody but Drew voted "Aye," and Daniel Drew was declared out of the road. Daniel was permitted to hold on to his profits, but Gould and Fisk got the Erie. Vanderbilt had most of his money back and was glad to be rid of the whole gang.

Jim Fisk was rather depressed at the prospect of being left nothing but the shell of the good old ship. With the seven million gone from the Erie treasury, Erie did not seem so attractive as when Drew had it. "Yes," said he, "the pirates have gone off with the swag, and left us nothing but the confounded hulk."

"Don't you mind," said Jay. "There may be some service left in the old ship yet."

And indeed there was!

III

Vanderbilt's first serious defeat had a sobering effect. Perhaps it was his age or perhaps it was the specter of men like Jacob Little, who rose and throve only to fall in the end, that made him cautious. But certainly his attitude was changed, and with this change his dominance was gone. He decided that he was through with railroads for the time being. He would hold on to those he had but there would be no more attempts at grabbing new roads, particularly when men like Jay Gould were on the scene.

Only once more did Vanderbilt try to buck Jay Gould. He had given up hope of ever acquiring the Erie but he thought that there might be a chance to cut into their business. A large part of the business of both the New York Central, Vanderbilt's road, and the Erie, with Gould now at its head, came from the shipment of cattle coming on at Buffalo and headed for the New York market. The rate on both roads was $125 a carload. Vanderbilt reduced the rate to $100. Gould cut it to $75. The Central then went to $50 and Erie countered by offering to bring cattle down at $25. Vanderbilt's ire was aroused, and he told the officers of his road to put the rate down to $1 a carload. Gould couldn't go much lower and Vanderbilt felt pleased with himself. He had tamed Gould this time anyway. Or, at least, so he thought. For the Erie apparently gave up the fight and stopped carrying cattle while the New York Central road was doing a rushing business. But Vanderbilt soon discovered that once again he was on the losing end. For Jay Gould had, in the meantime, gone into the cattle business, bought up every head of stock to be had west of Buffalo and was shipping them over his competitor's lines at a dollar a carload. On the basis of Vanderbilt's almost free transportation Gould had made a neat turn on his cattle deal at the Commodore's expense. Vanderbilt threw up his hands and gave up the fight. "Gould is the smartest man in America," he said. Either that was true or Caesar was getting old.

THE ERIE RAIDS

He was certainly showing his age at last for he began to express fear of these "fruitful noddles" of Jay Gould and his group. He began to spend most of his time in strange company. The office of New York's only female brokers, Woodhull and Claflin, was his usual retreat. It was there that Victoria Woodhull and Tennessee Claflin transacted business under the protection of a conspicuous sign:

ALL GENTLEMEN

WILL STATE THEIR BUSINESS

AND

THEN RETIRE AT ONCE

Vanderbilt found female company more interesting than new ventures and gradually his force as a market leader waned. When his son William suggested an extension of railroad interests his reply was: "We've gone far enough. Buffalo's my limit. If we go on West to Chicago, we might as well go clear to 'Frisco and China." Strange words for the man who had extended his shipping interests around the world and had not let men or governments stand in his way. He had lost only about $2,000,000 in the Erie wars but he began to fear for his large fortune. In the panic of 1873 he went in and supported the market. But this was only a defensive manoeuvre to protect his present interests and maintain his fortune intact. The maintenance rather than the extension of his fortune now became his chief aim. He was going fast and he knew it. In the panic of 1873 he was eighty years old. Money could do little for him now, but its possession had become a symbol and economy a habit. A doctor prescribed champagne in a serious illness. "Oh, no, doctor," he said, "I can't afford champagne! Won't soda water do?" In his last years the picturesque Commodore became obsessed with the idea of perpetuating his name and his deeds. The colossal vanity of the man was never better illustrated than by his proposal to the city government that it erect statues of Washington and himself, side by side, in Central Park. Indeed, during his lifetime, he was successful in securing the erection of a memorial in one of the smaller parks.

He held on a few years longer. On January 3, 1877, he finally loosened his hold on his $90,000,000, and found his peace. To Jay Gould and his crowd it meant little; they had never had much love for the fighting giant, and since they had beaten and cowed him they had had little fear.

CHAPTER VII

DREW TRIES TO COME BACK

FOR a while, after being forced out of the Erie by Gould and Fisk, the "speculative director" led a quiet and retired life. He was over seventy now and he decided to devote his time and his $13,000,000 to religious devotion and peaceful enjoyment. For a time he kept to his resolution. But out in the country it took a day longer to get the quotations, and with so many things happening in the Street it wasn't much fun out of the thick of it. Uncle Daniel decided to move into town again and see if he couldn't get up a deal with Gould and Fisk. They were the leaders in the market now and, in spite of the late disagreement between Drew and the others over the Erie spoils, he was anxious to be in with them, for they seemed to be on the right road to profits, and besides they had the Erie in hand. Drew didn't relish being treated like an outsider when it came to juggling the stock of the old stand-by.

Drew volunteered to help the others in whatever they were planning and, since the $13,000,000 at his disposal was real money, Gould and Fisk agreed to take Drew in on their present operation. Their plan was to sell Erie and other stocks short and then to force a general market decline by withdrawing large amounts of money from the market in actual currency and force interest rates up. Fisk and Gould together put up $10,000,000 and Drew, $4,-000,000 and the plan was started. The market was in the very middle of a boom and the public was buying stocks in large quantities. Money was easy, times were good and a strong market was the result. The pool sold stocks heavily short. In the meantime they had put the $14,000,000 into various banks. These banks had made loans against this reserve, of course, and had put the deposited funds into circulation. After the pool's short line was out the group went to the banks and had their checks for the entire amount of their deposit certified. Against these certified checks Gould and his crowd borrowed greenbacks which they immediately withdrew from circulation. This was all done so suddenly that the banks were forced to call their loans to brokers in order to protect their depleted reserves. The sudden drain on the money market of so large an amount forced up the call loan rate immediately. Money shot up to 160 per cent and brokers were unable to carry securities for their customers on any reasonable basis. Liquidation at once came in and stocks began to tumble. The effect of this sudden liquidation by the public became cumulative and there was a severe drop in stock prices. Thus far the operation had been immediately successful and Gould wanted to continue it further and put on the screws so tightly that the short pool would be able to net a profit even greater than the thirty-point drop in a few days would give them. Drew became worried and expressed fear at the public reaction to this move. Gould and Fisk were irritated at his timidity and released him from the pool. For themselves, they held on and planned to further the stringency of money by a new campaign.

The lock-up of money, a tremendous amount at that time, had seriously interfered not only with the stock market but with general credit conditions. Large business men in New York put pressure on the Secretary of the Treasury to release some of the currency in reserve in Washington and relieve the credit strain. Secretary McCulloch finally decided to do this. At this point, without letting Drew know anything of their plans, Gould and Fisk suddenly reversed their position, covered all their commitments and became bulls.

Old Dan Drew thought they were still on the short side, and after his retirement from the pool started a campaign on his own behalf. In spite of all his resolutions to retire he just couldn't keep out of the market, and now, with prices tumbling under forced selling, it seemed like a good time for a turn in Erie. Although Gould and Fisk, closely in touch with every operation, knew that he was selling short, Drew did not know that they had reversed their position in the market and were gobbling up every share of Erie in sight. It was not long before Gould and Jubilee Jim had bought up the whole floating supply of Erie, and Drew found himself seventy thousand shares short. Then Gould gave the signal to begin the squeeze. Erie jumped from 35 to 47 in a day. In three days more it was 57 and Drew was in a fix. The day after it was 62 and Drew knew that he was cornered. The source of the operation for the rise was now public information and Drew went to see Gould and Fisk. Certainly, he thought, they might let him out lightly. He had worked the settlement trick with Vanderbilt often, but this clique was not so easy to handle. Drew pleaded with them as old friends and partners. "Dan Drew," said Jim Fisk, "you are the last man in the world to whine over any position in which you may find yourself in Erie." Drew threatened to go to court, but they laughed.

The next day Drew actually appeared in court and petitioned to have the Erie put into receiver's hands. Among his arguments was this affidavit:

"Gould and Fisk have recently been engaged in locking up money; they told me so; they wanted me to join them in locking up money, and I did to the extent of $1,000,000, and refused to lock up any more; I had originally agreed to lock up $4,000,000, but when money became very tight, I deemed it prudent to decline to go any further and unlocked my million; the object of locking up is to make money scarce—to make stocks fall because people couldn't get the money to carry them.

Daniel Drew."

DREW TRIES TO COME BACK

This legal step was useless. The courts refused to aid Drew and indeed small chance he had. For by now Gould had made Bill Tweed and Peter Sweeney, the political bosses of New York, directors in the Erie. Gould further threatened that unless Drew settled at once without any more ado, he would put Erie up to a hundred. Drew knew he meant it and meekly covered his short sales, taking a loss of almost two million dollars.

Drew apparently did not have the good sense to keep out of Gould's way even after this costly operation. He would have done well to follow Vanderbilt's hands-off policy after his disastrous set-to, but Drew didn't know when he had met his match.

Vanderbilt issued a public statement about this time, in answer to a query as to his connection with Gould: "I have had but one business transaction with Mr. Gould in my life. . . . Since then I have had nothing to do with him in any way whatever; nor do I mean ever to have, except it be to defend myself." Vanderbilt accepted the situation and kept his money. Drew came out once more for battle and went bankrupt. What encouraged the old gentleman was a successful, if comparatively small, operation he conducted against Gould and Henry Smith. They had been selling Erie short for a quick turn but Drew, acting with a German banker who controlled a large part of the foreign supply, had put up the stock and squeezed Gould and Smith. They took a slight loss but Gould set out to get Drew and hurt him badly. He dropped in on Drew one day and suggested their joining in a bull operation in Erie. This pleased Uncle Dan and he jumped at the chance. For a while things went smoothly, but suddenly the stock weakened. Gould was selling Drew out but he professed to be mystified by the turn of events. He suggested holding on and at the same time sell Northwestern short. This latter had had a phenomenal rise. The idea was to make twelve or fifteen points on Northwestern and then go back to Erie after giving it a chance to settle. All this time Gould was selling Erie and was in a powerful pool to boost Northwestern. Henry Smith, Jay Gould's first partner in Wall Street, had also been told by Gould to sell Northwestern. When both stocks were going the wrong way, it became apparent that Gould was not on the level and Smith, who knew a great deal about Gould's activities, got a warrant for Gould's arrest on the charge of having looted the Erie treasury. Gould squirmed out of the charge but this step on Smith's part made him furious. From a mild squeeze, as he originally planned, he decided to turn his operation into a ruinous one for Drew and Smith. Northwestern was sent up to 150 then 160. At this price all the shorts except Drew and Smith were permitted to settle. These two would have to pay more, Drew because he had operated against Gould and Smith on account of his attempt at legal intervention. The stock was cornered and Gould could set the price. He made it 230 and told Drew and Smith to step up and settle. They were both cornered, having followed Gould's advice to sell short. Drew raised a public howl but even the newspapers did not help him. One New York paper said: "We cannot affect to have any sympathy with these men, and least of all with Drew. He has been one of the curses of the market for years past. If he has now received such a blow as will result in his being driven from the Street altogether no one will be sorry for him." Appeals to Gould, the newspapers, the courts, were equally hopeless. The squeeze put a still larger hole in Drew's pocket and made him more vulnerable than ever. As for Henry Smith, it forced him forever from the Street.

Things turned rapidly against Drew. On top of two disastrous blows from Gould his other opponents took courage and instituted suit on the basis of his stock issues when he was Treasurer of the Erie fifteen years back. Then again, the panic of 1873 found the brokerage firm of Kenyon, Cox and Company, of which he was chief owner, hopelessly involved. He tried to make a few quick turns but his touch was gone. Feather by feather they plucked the old bird. And pretty soon the "Big Bear," once the most powerful man on the Street, was declared bankrupt. At eighty, his property was listed as:

Watch and chain $150
Sealskin coat 150
Wearing apparel ....₁·₂... 100
Bible, hymn books, etc. 130

Even at that age and in that condition the old hanker-
ing for Wall Street remained. With the ticker now of
academic interest only, he found life dull. He still had
his hymn books, and, covered deep under four blankets,
even on the hottest days, he read and read and prepared himself to meet his Lord.

CHAPTER VIII

THE GOLD CONSPIRACY AND BLACK FRIDAY

SINCE the genius of Alexander Hamilton had put the country on a substantial monetary basis, the financial measures of the government had been conservative, so that fluctuations in currency had been practically eliminated. The doubtful financial measures of Congress in issuing irredeemable paper currency during the Civil War created a situation encouraging once more to speculation in money. A new form of trading came into being, that of speculation in government notes, or what amounts to the same thing, their equivalent in gold. In fact so extensive did trading in gold soon become, that for a time it dominated the speculative market and overshadowed the ordinary stock speculation.

The first issue of irredeemable paper currency, known as greenbacks, was made in February, 1862, to the amount of $150,000,000. This was followed in July by an additional issue of $150,000,000. Additional issues in the next year brought the total above $400,000,000. These greenbacks had only such value as the credit of the Union government could supply. They were, therefore, subject to fluctuation with every success or defeat of the

Union arms and the certainty or doubtfulness of their ultimate redemption. That such redemption could not be accepted as certain during these trying times can well be realized from the fact that the Confederate notes became valueless, as more recently, the notes of many European governments. A fall in greenbacks is the equivalent of a rise in gold and these fluctuations were necessary concomitants of the unstable situation. What aggravated the condition was the fact that large speculators artificially manipulated the rise and fall in quotations and that the violent fluctuations attracted so much public participation.

In uncertain periods the speculative public fever assumes an extreme degree. The whole population of the North gave itself up to a speculative frenzy. In the words of Medberry: "Everybody made ventures. Gold was the favorite with ladies. Clergymen affected mining stock and petroleum. Lawyers had a penchant for Erie. Solid merchants, preferring their customary staples, sold cotton or corn for future delivery or bought copper and salt on margin."

Trading in gold first started on the floor of the Stock Exchange in 1861. The leading brokers were skeptical as to its patriotic implications, since every purchase of gold, which meant an equivalent sale of greenbacks, was a definite indication of distrust of the nation's credit. The Governors of the Stock Exchange, actuated by patriotic motives, and influenced also by the fact that trading in securities was large enough to occupy the members, abolished all trading in gold on the floor after only a few months of activity. That wherever commissions can be made brokers will trade is an evident truth. The ruling that these trades could not be made on the floor of the Stock Exchange succeeded only in transferring the business to other agencies.

An open air market had recently been organized in William Street, between Exchange Place and Beaver Street. It differed from the Curb Market of our days in that the same stocks which sold on the floor were also traded in here. This curb market was active only during the period of the day when calls on the Exchange board were suspended and therefore gave traders a continuous market. It was to this market that the gold trading was first brought after its exclusion from the Stock Exchange.

By 1862 the Coal Hole had been established as an additional trading center. A basement at No. 23 William Street was rented by an enterprising individual who charged a small fee for entrance. Gold dealing was the main feature of the Coal Hole. In 1863 Gilpin's news room at the southeast corner of William Street and Exchange Place was converted into a trading room for gold, and $25 a year admittance fee was charged each member. All of this trading was ostensibly in gold but the effect was, of course, gambling on the Government's ability and willingness to redeem the greenbacks. Quotations were in terms of gold, but this stable metal is almost stationary in value, and it was the conversion of greenbacks into gold which was actually the fluctuating factor.

Speculation in stocks, unfortunate as it may be to any individual, is a necessary adjunct to a capitalistic organization of industrial society. Purchases of commodities and staples for future delivery are a method of insurance for the merchant. These have their economic justification. Speculation in gold had no basis in necessity, except for the small amount that merchants required to fill anticipated foreign payments. That this form of trading reached such tremendous volume during and just after the Civil War is merely evidence of the speculative propensities of the American public. And strangely enough it was in speculative ventures in gold that the lay individual was at the greatest disadvantage, for the fluctuations in greenbacks were dependent largely upon the fortunes of the Union Army. Victories or defeats were known to the large operators through representatives on the ground and by arrangement with government officials long before the newspapers printed them. Even the ordinary chances of the outsider were minimized in this form of trading. And once again, as in the period after the Revolution, public officials were involved. It was alleged that a member of the Cabinet, whose position naturally enabled him to get news in advance of the public, made a fortune by telegraphing his

THE GOLD ROOM

THE REGULAR BOARD

brokers to sell or buy gold, depending on the information he had of the success of the Union forces. His brokers carried his account without capital in exchange for
being relayed the news before it was released to the
newspapers. As a matter of fact the quotations in gold
were used as a quicker messenger and more accurate
reflection of successes or defeats of the Union Army
than were the news dispatches of the Associated Press.

Gold first went to a premium on April 18, 1862, when
it was quoted at 101½. By July 21st it stood at 120.
Secretary Chase did all he could to stop trading and
arrest the drop in greenbacks but it was useless. By 1863
gold went to 169. In 1864 Chase decided to support the
government currency by selling gold at 165 and thus
force up the price of greenbacks. This step halted the
rise in gold for a short time, but its only permanent influence was that it shook the security market also, and
bankrupted Anthony Morse, Sam Hallett and many
smaller operators and firms who were carrying on bull
operations in the stock market. Chase's campaign was
powerless to arrest the rise of gold and it was soon 182.
On July 11th, gold reached its highest quotation, selling
at 285. All this time a tremendous volume of trading had
been carried on in Gilpin's and the Coal Hole. In October, 1864, a new Gold Board was formed by a more
substantial group and took up its quarters at 24 Beaver
Street. The Gold Board, because of its sponsorship, drew
the major part of the trading away from the smaller

independent exchanges, and several large operators were attracted by the manipulative possibilities. The days apparently were too short for the gold speculators and they were accustomed to meet evenings in the corridors of the Fifth Avenue Hotel. A Mr. Gallagher diverted the group by opening an evening exchange in a room back of the hotel, and until midnight the calls of quotations were mingled with the other strange noises of New York's night life.

With every successive victory of the Union forces, gold receded and gradually approached normal. Sherman's successful march to the sea brought gold to 147, and for some time thereafter fluctuations were very slight. Outside speculation became smaller with the stabilization and soon after the end of the war most of the brokers deserted the Gold Board. From then until 1869 trading in gold was within narrow margins. In that year, the Gold Board was to witness its most dramatic episode as a prelude to its final collapse.

II

In 1869 the Government held between $75,000,000 and $100,000,000 in gold. The floating market supply was about $20,000,000 and it was on the basis of this supply that the trading was done in the Gold Room. To the fertile mind of Jay Gould the idea occurred that this supply could be cornered and a tremendous profit made by tying it up and holding it at an inflated price. At this time there were two classes of purchasers in the market: those buying for legitimate export, and those purchasing or selling short for purely speculative purposes. If a stock could be cornered, as had often been done, then it was possible also to corner gold. Or, at least, so Jay Gould thought. The profit of a successful operation in gold had much greater possibilities. There was, however, one consideration implicit in such a coup that did not need to be considered in a stock corner. During the operation it was necessary to insure against having the Government throw any of its gold on the market and break the corner. Besides the other usual precautions it was therefore necessary for Gould to get the co-operation of important Government officials. In some way he must reach the President of the United States. Having outlined his program, Gould set about to make it effective.

Late in May, 1869, Jay Gould made a social visit to Abel Rathbone Corbin who, some months before at the age of 67, had crowned a successful career as a lawyer, speculator and lobbyist, by marrying President Grant's sister. Corbin was very close to Grant and was reputed to have great influence on his opinion. It was Grant's custom to stay at Corbin's home when visiting New York and the co-operation of Corbin in the scheme might solve the problem of government co-operation or at least prevent interference. Among other things discussed by the two men was the price of gold. Either because of Gould's logical reasoning or Corbin's desire to share in the booty the visit was eminently successful. Before Gould left it was arranged that he was to purchase for Corbin's account $1,500,000 of gold at 133 without any payment on Corbin's part. It was also arranged that on President Grant's next visit to New York Gould was to be Corbin's guest at his home and have the opportunity, as a public-spirited citizen, of discussing with Grant the important national question of the price of gold and its effect on the country's industrial development.

Gould quietly began purchasing gold in the open market in large quantities in anticipation of the maturity of his plans. On June 15, 1869, President Grant came to New York and Gould met him at Corbin's home. The occasion was purely social but successful to the extent that Grant accepted an invitation to attend a performance at Jim Fisk's theatre. He sat in Fisk's private box and it was arranged for him to take a trip next evening to Newport on Fisk's private boat. Fisk was not yet in on the details of the gold manipulation but he had an inkling that some large project was under way and readily joined Gould in entertaining Grant. Cyrus W. Field and several other prominent individuals in the confidence of Gould were also invited. The party was very informal. Fisk, as master of ceremonies, enjoyed himself hugely, and, although he didn't know

CYRUS W. FIELD

*He began life as a rag merchant, laid the first Atlantic
cable, went into Wall Street, became a millionaire,
and lived his last years dependent upon the
charity of his friends.*

exactly what it was all about, felt that something was going to be "put over" and was glad to be in on it. At dinner the conversation was adroitly turned to the question of the price of gold. Grant's opinion was directly asked but his answer was evasive and disappointing. Gould later testified that it was like a "wet blanket" on his plans. The time for intensive action had apparently not yet arrived, and Gould, ever patient, decided to wait until he was absolutely certain of Grant's reaction.

The time between June and August was used by Gould to accumulate more gold and to solidify his position. One of the important financial posts in the United States was the Assistant Treasurership at New York. Through this official government gold was sold on the Gold Exchange and the proper man in that place could supply valuable aid and information. Through the influence of Corbin an acceptable man was appointed in the person of General Butterfield. In the meantime, Dominick Henry, an Englishman of excellent reputation as an authority on financial problems, was engaged to prepare for Gould extensive reports and analyses of the effect of a rise in the price of gold on the economic condition of the country. These articles were run in magazines and newspapers throughout the United States. Hundreds of persons of different walks of life were posted where they would come into contact with Grant and be able to give him their views on the question of the Government policy in relation to gold, views which were the carefully rehearsed opinions of Gould. At almost every public dinner or political meeting Grant attended, the subject was brought up and Gould's viewpoint impressed upon Grant. Everywhere Grant went he heard Gould's opinion echoed. This man of action was exceedingly naïve in most things. He was very much impressed by this well-organized propaganda and in the honesty of his simplicity he began to believe that Gould was right.

On Sept. 2, 1869, the President came again to New York to stay at Corbin's home. After his departure Corbin immediately reported to Gould that Grant had finally come over to Gould's opinion, and had, when at Corbin's house, dispatched a letter to Secretary of the Treasury Boutwell directing him not to sell any Government gold without specific instructions from him. It was the signal for Gould to set the trap.

When Gould had started buying gold in June, it was at 130. It was up to 133 when Corbin's gold was purchased and had fluctuated only slightly afterwards. With the information of Grant's unwitting co-operation in the manoeuvre, Gould set about buying gold heavily. By the 7th of September gold was up to 137, and Gould handed Corbin a check for $25,000 as a token of his appreciation and an advance on his profits. Corbin was consistently modest about having his name mentioned in these operations and the check was made out in blank.

All this time Gould was working alone although other

brokers were following his movements and buying along with him. Gould had full knowledge of the action of the other buyers and, while not co-operating, encouraged the purchases. Gold was being bought in large quantities, but by skillful placing of orders the price was kept from severe fluctuations until the time for the push arrived. About the tenth of the month Gould's plans began to meet difficulties. The shorts, who had been selling gold consistently, headed by James Brown and Henry Clews, showed unexpected power and signs of organization against Gould.

Gould was getting a bit worried and decided to take Fisk in as an active worker in the operation. On the 15th of the month he disclosed his plans to Fisk. About that time he also purchased for the account of General Butterfield, Assistant Treasurer at New York, $1,500,-000 of gold. This was carried for Butterfield without any contribution on his part and, while it was probably not done at his request, was done with his knowledge. A letter was also sent to General Porter, private secretary to President Grant, informing him that $500,000 of gold had been purchased for his account, but this transaction was repudiated by Porter.

The political details having been arranged as completely as possible, Gould set about perfecting the financial operations. The purchases of gold would tie up a great deal of money and Gould was not the man to freeze any more funds than absolutely necessary. The

Tenth National Bank, under the control of Boss Tweed, began to function for the conspirators. Gould had not been in the bank more than three or four times previously but in his present manipulation he saw the possibility of using its machinery to aid his plans. In giving deposits as guarantee against his purchases of gold, Gould planned to use certified checks of the bank which he arranged to be issued regardless of the amount of his deposits. It was an easy way of carrying his gold without putting up real cash and the Tenth National became a manufactory of certified checks.

Things then began to move rapidly although not altogether smoothly. Grant came to New York again on September 10th and stayed until the 13th. Gould saw him once more and even the simple Grant began to be suspicious. The operator was perhaps too insistent and Grant complained to Corbin that Gould always seemed to be trying to get something out of him. On the 13th Grant left for Washington, Pa., for a rest. Gould was getting a bit nervous and wanted to make absolutely sure of Grant's attitude before the final attack. He had Corbin write a letter to Grant, which was dispatched by special messenger, urging Grant not to permit the sale of Government gold under any circumstances. It was a great mistake on Gould's part and the situation must indeed have been serious to make the careful financier venture such an obvious manoeuvre. The letter was opened by General Porter, who was with Grant. Porter's suspicions were immediately aroused, particularly in view of the fact that the clique had tried to get him to accept the purchase of $500,000 in gold. Porter communicated his suspicions to President Grant and prevailed upon him to stop Corbin's association with Gould. Mrs. Grant thereupon wrote a letter to Mrs. Corbin telling her that the President had heard rumors that Corbin was speculating in Wall Street. Should this be the case, Mrs. Grant wrote, the President desired an immediate disconnection with any operations on Corbin's part.

About the same time Gould made another serious mistake of judgment. He wrote directly to Secretary Boutwell pointing out the advantages of a premium on gold and suggesting an increase in the amount the Government was carrying. Not satisfied with some assurance that the Government would not sell he proposed that the Secretary of the Treasury buy more gold on behalf of the Government. Boutwell was at no time sympathetic with either Gould or his viewpoint and it was a rash and useless thing to do. The letter put Boutwell on his guard and made him all the more favor the bears who were now actively and openly favoring the sale of large quantities of gold by the Government.

The letter from Mrs. Grant to Mrs. Corbin frightened Corbin. On September 22nd, he showed the letter to Gould and told him that he must withdraw entirely from the operation. It was somewhat of a shock to

Gould. He tried to persuade Corbin to stay in by promise of further reward but the old lobbyist was thoroughly
scared and could not be prevailed upon under any circumstances. Corbin suggested that Gould take the gold
held in his name, for which he had never paid, off his
hands at the market price. His paper profits on that day
were $100,000 and he asked Gould for that amount.
Gould asked time to think it over. If Corbin withdrew
his co-operation, or if the letter was seen by a single
bear, the game was up. The next morning Gould saw
Corbin and told him he could give him nothing if he
withdrew, but if he stayed in he could have Gould's
check for $100,000. Corbin, however, was thoroughly
frightened by the complications Gould had brought him
into and refused to have any further connection with
the business.

Gould had been operating through several firms. One
of them alone had accumulated $50,000,000 for his ac-
count. As the total market supply amounted to only
about $20,000,000 it meant that the opposition had
sold a tremendous amount which they could not deliver.
If there was no hitch in the operation Gould could
squeeze the shorts and force them to cover at his own
price. But, unfortunately, Corbin's withdrawal was final
and complete. Gould's connection with Washington was
destroyed and the corner might be broken at any moment by Government intervention and sale of their
gold. Gould was now in a fix. He knew that the Govern-

ment might sell any day and that he must do something quickly or otherwise he might be saddled with $100,000,-000 in gold on a falling market. To sell that amount in a day or two without breaking the price was impossible. The shorts, meanwhile, encouraged by news from Washington, were confident and not hastening to cover. Jim Fisk was called in. Without being given any reasons, he was told to go on the floor the next day and put gold up to a hundred and sixty no matter how much he had to take up. If anything happened Gould would take care of him. He was also told to give his orders to as many different brokers as possible, all to buy, and give verbal orders only. Gould was out to make a market for his $100,000,000 of gold.

This was Thursday, October 2, 1869. In two hours Gould sold more than $50,000,000 of gold. No one knew who was selling and the largest purchasers were Jim Fisk and Albert Speyer, Fisk's chief broker. It was Gould's crowd, apparently, that was buying, and the other bulls, who tagged along after the great operator, were encouraged by this display of power. By the close of the day Gould had managed to sell his $100,000,000 in gold at top prices mainly because Fisk had created the market. Fisk, Speyer, Belden and the rest of Gould's own pool had, strangely enough, been the principal purchasers.

That evening there was a meeting of the members of the clique. Gould attended but said not a word about his sales. The group decided to bring their original scheme to a head. They had gold enough, as they supposed, absolutely to control the market. To-morrow, Friday, they planned to press the price to the utmost and compel settlement at their figures.

The next day, October 4, 1869, will always be remembered as Black Friday. Fisk was at his office early across the street from the Gold Room. Jay Gould came down town that day determined not to utter an unnecessary word. He knew what would happen; he knew that the day's upheaval would shake the very foundations of the Gold Exchange. He determined to keep quiet and his directions were nods and whispers. On the most exciting day of the Exchange's history the central figure sat huddled in a chair, alone, tearing up bits of paper. Not a word, not a gesture, betrayed his feelings or his plans.

The floor of the Exchange was in a panic at the very opening. Jim Fisk paraded around offering to bet $50,-000 that gold would reach 200. It kept going up steadily —from 145 it leaped at a bound to 150. Buy, buy, buy! shouted Jim Fisk, and his brokers offered 150, 155, 160. Half a million went at 160. By 11 o'clock the excitement had reached outside the Exchange. Crowds had collected on the street. Inside the floor was quiet as a grave one moment and wild with excitement the next. Fisk, back at his office, rushed around, yelling orders, calling himself the Napoleon of Wall Street, swearing at his brokers

—and always buying. Gould was quiet and calm and silent. He was waiting for the inevitable crash.

Again Fisk was on the floor. "161 for any part of $5,000,000!" His offers to buy became louder and more defiant. There were no sellers. "162 for $5,000,000!" A quiet voice replied, "Sold at 162." It was James Brown, the Scottish banker and leader of the opposition. Suddenly word spread around the floor that Secretary Boutwell would sell. There were whispers, conferences. Another sale at 162, and the next moment came a telegraphic order from Washington—the Government was selling! The bubble had burst. Brokers were left struggling among themselves as the leaders left for hurried conferences; like riderless horses the small brokers milled about trying to execute cancelled orders. In one corner of the room Fisk's brokers were bidding 160 while gold was offered at 140. Albert Speyer went crazy. He marched around the floor shouting "Shoot me! Shoot me!" as he yelled his offers to buy at 160, 170, 180. Before the gong had sounded, gold was back to 135. Black Friday was over. Gould had failed—but he had not lost.

The end of the day had brought the end of the Gold Exchange. The shock of Black Friday ruined hundreds of firms and thousands of individuals. The name of Jay Gould became in the public mind a synonym for organized greed and ruthless rapacity. This did not please Jay but it could not be helped; a man's work must be done regardless of what the masses think.

[165]

Gould had got out in time, and with a handsome profit, but Jim Fisk was hopelessly involved. He had purchased such enormous amounts of gold that meeting his obligations was impossible. In the Erie Railroad mansion, under heavy guard, Jay Gould and Jim Fisk conferred as Jay worked out the plan for covering Fisk.

The plan finally decided upon was this: Fisk was to repudiate all purchases made by Belden and Speyer, his chief brokers, the brokers to accept all the purchases on their account and declare themselves bankrupt. As compensation Gould would give each of them an income for life. This would not please the Street but not a single paper could be produced showing Fisk's written orders, and in New York City, land of the Tweed, Fisk's word was more effective than the law.

David Dudley Field, the eminent lawyer, who dimmed a brilliant career by his association with Tweed and Gould, was called in to manage the legal end. Bill Tweed got busy, and instructed the always purchasable Judge Barnard to report at Jim Fisk's office at once. There, under Gould's dictation, Barnard issued injunctions restraining sundry and all persons from enforcing sundry and all contracts not at present agreeable to Jay Gould. Not a single contract could be enforced against Jim Fisk. The court calendars were clogged for years with the cases centering around the Gold Conspiracy. But Tweed was the local government, and his word was precedent, law and decision. Jay Gould held on to his gains and not James Brown nor all the Scottish bankers in the world could make him disgorge.

Even as judged by the doubtful ethics of the financial giant of the period, this ingenious method of squirming out of a tight fix put Gould in a bad light. Other firms lost millions by this transaction although their books showed profits. Only from Speyer and Belden could the losses be recovered legally. And these men and their firms were hopelessly bankrupt. The matter even reached Congress, as all things ultimately do, and there it was buried. Investigation followed investigation and all that was determined was that Gould had broken his own market. He had deliberately set out to topple the structure he himself so carefully created in order to save himself and, as Jim Fisk put it, "Let every one carry out his own corpse."

III

Jay Gould's coup in the gold market, incomplete as it was, was none the less disastrous to the banking fraternity and the general public. For the public Jay Gould became the symbol of evil incarnate. Jim Fisk, perhaps because of his jovial personality, was more gently treated. A press campaign, headed by Samuel Bowles of the Springfield *Republican* and James Gordon Bennett of the New York *Herald*, gave Gould a reputation for diabolic evil that he never lived down. The public not only disliked Gould but began to fear him, and this attitude gave his enemies courage.

And just at this time, when Gould was on the defensive, Jim Fisk, his loyal ally, died. That supreme mountebank of fortune, in the words of Henry Ward Beecher, "the glaring meteor, abominable in his lusts, and flagrant in his violation of public decency," who had stood between Jay Gould and the public, was shot down by a rival in a quarrel over the notorious show girl, Josie Mansfield. One of the two young pirates, whom Fagin Drew had carefully taught and who in turn had caused his ruin, was gone. Jay Gould remained, but his enemies, increasing in number and in courage, were on his trail.

It has already been noted that a large proportion of the Erie railroad stock was held in England. Taking advantage of the aroused public sentiment in America, the English capitalists combined with Gould's opponents in the United States in a determined effort to oust Gould and regain control of the Erie. They carefully formed their offensive and engaged General Daniel E. Sickles, one of the heroes of Gettysburg and then Minister to Spain, to lead the fight. He secured leave of absence from his diplomatic duties and sailed for the States. Here he enlisted as aides General John A. Dix, later Governor of New York, General George B. McClellan and William R. Travers. This imposing group at once opened fire.

Canvassing the officers, they brought to their side Vice President Archer of the Erie, who had succeeded Fisk.

W. R. TRAVERS

*The senior partner in the famous business and social
alliance of Travers and Jerome.*

Archer, in turn, won over several members of the Board of Directors. They immediately called upon Gould to hold a special meeting. Gould paid no attention. Archer thereupon called the meeting and prepared to take possession of the Erie offices by force. The Grand Opera House at 23rd Street and Eighth Avenue, New York, housed the Erie offices, in close proximity to Fisk's theatre and several residences. Gould barricaded the building and stationed armed pickets at the entrance. The storming forces finally gained entrance to the building but not to the private offices. They did manage to get hold of a great many of the record books and a careful perusal immediately revealed facts which would not sound well in a court of law. When Gould was confronted with this material his opposition immediately weakened. They could send him to jail and he knew it. After a feeble gesture, offering to leave all matters in dispute to Horace Greeley, he decided to abdicate—on favorable terms. An armistice was declared to draw up a treaty of peace, pending which Gould retired as president, leaving the office to General Dix.

Suit was instituted against Gould for $12,803,059, which amount he was accused of transferring from the Erie treasury to his personal account. This suit was held over Gould's head during the negotiations. In the meantime Dix had been elected Governor of New York State and a man named Watson was made President of the Erie. Horace F. Clark was a close friend of both Gould and Watson, and he took a hand in the negotiations towards reparations. It was finally agreed that Gould was to make restitution in part on condition that the criminal charges be withdrawn.

Here was a new situation and every new situation meant a new possibility for profit to the wily Gould. He was now out of the Erie, but he meant to take his final leave under favorable auspices and in his accustomed style. The original righteous indignation had somewhat worn off as the virtuous generals in command had been diverted to other worthy efforts. Clark and Watson were more practical men and they entered into an arrangement with Gould to juggle the price of Erie stock on the basis of the settlement. One day it was reported that Gould intended to restore the plunder and Erie advanced. A day or two later there was a denial of the report; down came the price. This was repeated several times and with each announcement Gould and the others bought at the bottom and sold at the top. It was his farewell bow to the "Scarlet Woman of Wall Street."

Finally the restitution agreement was announced with a flourish. Gould was to turn over the Opera House and adjoining buildings held in his own name and, in addition, stocks to the par value of $6,000,000. That amount of stock was actually turned over by Gould but the lot was proved later to be worth not more than $200,000 on the market.

During Gould's administration of the road $64,000,-

ooo in stock had been issued. Not one dollar had been an addition to real investment. It was a great blow to Gould to be ousted from the road, for no longer would the trusty Erie furnish funds for all his many market enterprises. However, it wasn't fatal. As Jim Fisk would have put it, "Cheer up, my hearty! Nothing is lost save honor."

CHAPTER IX

MILLIONAIRES IN SUPPORT

IN market operations smaller in scope, but often as dramatic in their effects, were many minor operators who forged their way ahead for a time in the Civil War period. The names of the great leaders dwarf theirs, for powerful as some of these men became for a short period, either their judgment or their luck failed them at a crucial time.

Leonard W. Jerome was a keen market manipulator. Starting with very little, he gradually amassed a fortune, and then saw it disappear in a few weeks under the onslaught of an organized and powerful group. Jerome had just been admitted to the bar, when his brother, Addison G., persuaded him to give up the idea of practicing law and go into a newspaper venture with him. On borrowed capital they started a small daily in Rochester called *The Native American*. The enterprise did not prosper, and taking advantage of some political connections he had made during his brief experience in journalism, Leonard Jerome succeeded in securing appointment as Consul at Trieste. His brother in the meantime had entered the dry goods business. Along about 1854, Addi-

LEONARD W. JEROME

He made a fortune selling short.

son, the older of the two, invited his brother to join him as a partner, and Leonard Jerome resigned his post and sailed for the United States. While en route the firm failed and young Jerome arrived to find himself without a job. Looking around for something to do Jerome called on an old friend of the family. This man was then Treasurer of the Cleveland and Toledo Railroad, and Jerome solicited his influence in getting a connection. There was no job for Jerome, but this he did get—a sure tip to buy the stock of the Cleveland road. The source seemed to be authoritative, and Leonard Jerome made his first Wall Street venture by putting his total capital of $2,000 into the purchase of this stock. Jerome later claimed that the treasurer had been selling while he was giving his friends the advice to buy. In any case, the stock immediately started downward, and he lost $1,400 before it occurred to him that something was wrong. Jerome was disturbed but not discouraged. Putting aside a reserve of $100 against starvation, the young plunger deposited his remaining $500 with a broker and took another chance. This time he sold short and made a profit. He added the profit to his capital and sold again. With every new short sale he extended the scope of the operations and he was consistently successful. As his capital grew larger his profits increased proportionately. One misstep at this time, limited as was his capital, and involved as he was at every stage, might mean Jerome's finish. But the panic of 1857, coming as it did when Jerome had become a fairly large trader on the short side, made him a wealthy man. By the time the Civil War began he was one of the leading figures in the Street, and, in scattered operations, an ally of men like Vanderbilt and Drew. In 1863 Jerome started a stock brokerage firm with William R. Travers, a prominent broker and a social leader. He also took into the firm his older brother, Addison G. Jerome.

Vanderbilt became a customer of the new brokerage firm and took the three partners into his Harlem and Hudson corners. They all made a great deal of money supporting Vanderbilt. Addison did not hold on to his share long however. His success in the Vanderbilt syndicate, and in one or two other coups coming soon after, made him very confident of his manipulative ability. He had been in Wall Street only nine months when he went into a foolhardy operation against Henry Keep. Leonard was then in Europe and Addison was operating alone. His idea was to buy up control of the Michigan Southern Railroad in the open market. Henry Keep was then treasurer of the road and not enthusiastic over Addison's efforts. In the buying for control the stock had reached a very high figure, and Keep sold Addison Jerome all the stock he seemed to want. Jacob Little had long before opened the way to an easy method of securing stock for delivery. In the charter of the Michigan Southern was a clause permitting the Board of Directors to increase the capital stock at any time.

Keep controlled the board, and in a secret meeting the stock of the company was increased by 14,000 shares. In the meantime, Addison Jerome went on buying and sending up the price day by day. Jerome thought that he had most of the stock of the road, and began to prepare for a squeeze of the shorts preparatory to getting control of the road. He called for immediate delivery, and to his surprise, received at once all the stock he had purchased. The price of Michigan Southern had been lifted to an artificial level, and as soon as Addison Jerome realized the situation, the stock broke forty points in one day. Nine months before, Jerome had come into Wall Street with a few thousand dollars and good connections. In that period, by several lucky turns of a large order, he had been able to accumulate $3,000,000. The whole stake went into this one operation and Addison Jerome was out of Wall Street. The following year he died.

Leonard Jerome's success was not as short-lived. He was not as daring as his older brother but his smaller profits remained with him longer. After some minor successes he had extended his interests to real estate. Race tracks were his hobby and he built one of the finest in the country in Westchester, New York. Leonard Jerome was a clever floor trader and was often selected by pools to engineer their floor operations. A combination was formed in 1862 to bull Pacific Mail stock. In this pool were most of the directors of the line, who held

26,000 of the 40,000 shares outstanding. The pool transferred their stock to Brown Brothers and Company, to be held in trust for their benefit for five years. This step was taken to insure against having any of the group sell the others out. Then Leonard Jerome was called on to boost the price of the stock in the open market. This he did very successfully. In 1861 Pacific Mail was quoted at 69. Within eighteen months he had it up to 160. A group of shorts came in at this level, and Jerome put the stock up to 200 and forced them to settle. In 1865 Pacific Mail's stock was increased from $4,000,000 to $10,000,000, and the new stock was soon selling at 240, or the equivalent of 600 on the old stock. In 1866 the capital was increased again, this time to $20,000,-000. The new stock was quoted at 180, which meant an equivalent value of 900 on the old stock. All this time Jerome had been in charge, and although not a member of the pool, had been making a great deal of money by trading in Pacific Mail on his own account. In 1867 Jerome made a deal with the pool to buy all of its stock at 160 a share. Strange enough, as soon as the directors dissolved their combination, the published earnings of Pacific Mail began to show a serious decrease. A tremendous amount of "water" had been injected into the stock, and besides, the earnings statements had previously postponed or eliminated the showing of any unfavorable figures which sooner or later would have to be taken up in the accounts. As soon as the stock was loaded on Jerome the company did not hesitate to issue a report showing their assets reduced to $20,000,000 as compared with the previous figure of $34,000,000. At a meeting of the board soon after, in spite of Jerome's struggles, the dividend was reduced. A generally weak market did not help Jerome any, and a powerful short group organized to make a drive against Jerome. They broke Pacific Mail, and in a few days it dropped from 163 to 115. Whether the same directors who sold to Jerome were in this short group, is not known. The result to Jerome was, in any case, disastrous. For one week he struggled, raising every dollar he could to protect his holdings which he was carrying on margin. The opposition, however, was too powerful, and he was almost completely wiped out. Only a few parcels of real estate, which he fortunately had not been able to convert into cash to support his Pacific Mail holdings, were left to him. Remembering his brother's fate, Leonard Jerome left for Paris and kept his distance from Wall Street to the end of his days.

It is a curious fact that most of the operators in the class just below the great manipulative minds died bankrupt or nearly so. Apparently it is not only the ten-share trader who is finally squeezed out. Anthony Wellman Morse was one of the "big guns" in this category. In 1864 Morse was only thirty years old and had already survived two failures. In that year he attempted two unusual manipulative enterprises.

The first of these operations was in Chicago and Rock Island Railroad. In December, 1863, Morse went in with Thomas C. Durant, who had built the road, in a plan to advance the stock. By the end of the winter they had bought all of the 56,000 shares outstanding, and had options on a great deal of stock in addition. The price of stock was advanced from 107 to 150 by their buying activities, and it looked as though the shorts were cornered. Together with Morse and Durant three or four others had been admitted into the pool. Success for them seemed certain, as the shorts were beginning to cover at continually advancing prices, when Morse discovered that among the certificates that were being delivered to him were a great many that had been purchased for the pool account. One member of the pool had turned traitor. This discovery disrupted plans and prevented operations for a further rise. Afraid that this traitorous step might lead to a serious break in the price, Morse immediately decided to settle with the shorts at a small profit, and the abortive corner was over. This operation was moderately profitable to Morse despite the betrayal, and he decided to repeat it on a larger scale with the stock of the Pittsburgh, Fort Wayne and Chicago Railroad. He loaded himself up with this stock, and saw it go up from 56 to 153, in spite of a falling general market. Secretary of the Treasury Chase was at this time much concerned with the continual depression of greenbacks, and in order to

JOHN W. MACKAY

*The best known of the four Irishmen (three of them
former bartenders) who pooled their resources
and struck it rich in the Comstock lode.*

support the Government paper announced that he would sell gold. This step would be fatal to Morse's plans as he was in no position to boost, or even support, his huge quantity of stock in a falling market. He telegraphed to Washington that he was ready to buy all the gold the Government had to sell, but it was merely a gesture. Chase paid no attention to him and threw $9,000,000 in gold on the market, at the same time locking up greenbacks. Chase's announcement was made on Friday, April 15th. On Monday morning Fort Wayne stock, which closed on Saturday at 142, opened at 120. Two hours later the failure of Morse and Company was announced. At the same time Vanderbilt was staging his corner in Harlem successfully against the general market trend. But Anthony Morse was no Vanderbilt, and he went down and carried with him twelve other firms.

The Jerome brothers and Morse were all brilliant and daring operators. They went down because they attempted to carry too heavy a burden. Such was also the fate of William H. Marston, famous in his day for his Prairie du Chien corner. All of these had their brief period of glory in the Civil War period. There were others who came through, men like August Belmont, the Schell brothers, Henry Keep and John Tobin. The Western group of mining millionaires was also well known in Wall Street, but most of them did not endanger the money made in mining and railroads by manipulative operations. The four bright young Irish-men, three of them former bartenders, who pooled their resources and struck it rich from the Comstock Lode and held on to their money, pulled through. John W. Mackay, who later started the Mackay telegraph lines, James C. Flood, James G. Fair and W. S. O'Brien were the lucky four. Leland Stanford, Collis Hunting-ton, Darius Mills and Mark Hopkins became rich in railroad building in the Far West. But all these men were only incidentally connected with Wall Street. Per-haps that is the reason that they were able to hand on their money to their families instead of acting like Jerome, Morse, Marston and the others, merely as tem-porary holders. For in Wall Street the keen birds eat the worms but the bigger birds sometimes eat *them*.

CHAPTER X

JAY COOKE CRASHES

THE financial adolescence of the United States was now a thing of the past. But just as with humans, the rapid growth and the sudden change from youth to manhood were attended with excesses leading to internal disorders and complications. The railroads had spanned the continent. Every builder was ambitious to add a line to cement the connection. The late '60's and the early '70's witnessed a perfect fury of transcontinental building. Much of it was necessary, all of it was advisable. But a large part of it was inadequately financed, prematurely launched and unsubstantially planned. An era of untrammeled speculation had come in with the optimistic psychology of a never-ending prosperity. An inflated currency gave the illusion of easy money, and rapidly rising prices on the Stock Exchange invited extensive speculation by the public. The mania for speculation was in turn used by promoters to stimulate the distribution of their securities, and on this structure, ever weakening as its scope broadened, an unprecedented railway expansion was based.

[187]

Among the largest of the railroads built just before the panic of 1873 was the Northern Pacific. The bankers for this road were Jay Cooke and Company, whose reputation had been cemented by their appointment as Government financial agents during the Civil War. During the war this firm had successfully distributed for the government the famous 7–30 loan, so called because the bonds bore interest of 7 3/10ths per cent. In the financing of the Northern Pacific Jay Cooke conceived the idea of floating a 7–30 loan for his road, thus capitalizing his excellent reputation in connection with the government flotation. Although the issue was tremendous, so powerful was this financier's hold on the public imagination that thousands of ministers, school-teachers, widows and others of similar station, rarely associated in those times with Wall Street financing, joined in the investment opportunty. The Northern Pacific Railroad, said Jay Cooke, was "an enterprise which has never yet been excelled in the merits of its appeal to the public." But in spite of the wide public participation Jay Cooke found the outside funds insufficient to float the enterprise. A European syndicate which had subscribed for a large block, cancelled its subscription in 1872 because of the outbreak of the Franco-Prussian War. The Credit Mobilier scandals had made another part of the public cautious in its commitments. Cooke's heart was in his huge enterprise, and he did not delay continuance of building to await completion of his financing. His firm's

WALL STREET IN 1870

On the extreme right is the modest home of the
Dupont Gunpowder Company.

resources went into the railroad pending public participation and the credit of Jay Cooke and Company was stretched to a dangerous point.

In August, 1873, Daniel Drew's firm, Kenyon, Cox and Company, became involved, both because of Drew's personal manipulations and because of the failure of the Canada Southern Railway, whose paper they had carried in large quantities. On September 17th, money climbed to 25 per cent, but the public attitude was still bullish. The New York *Herald*, after this warning rumble, commented as follows: "Never before have such opportunities for investment been offered." But meanwhile, Jay Cooke's firm was tottering. A rumor to this effect was started in the Street but it was promptly denied. The fact was hard to believe for it sounded to the public of that day as if we of to-day were told that J. P. Morgan and Company were on the brink of failure.

On Sept. 18, 1873, at 12:15 P. M., a clerk came out of the offices of Jay Cooke and Company in Philadelphia and posted this notice on the front door of the building:

September 18, 1873.

TO THE PUBLIC—We regret to be obliged to announce that, owing to unexpected demands on us our firm has been obliged to suspend payment. In a few days we will be able to present a statement to our creditors, until which time we must ask their patient consideration. We believe our assets to be largely in excess of our liabilities.

Jay Cooke & Co.

This was the beginning of the end. The Northern Pacific was a $100,000,000 venture. Its securities had been placed in the homes of every strata of the population. Not only financiers, but the humblest individuals were directly affected. Public apprehension added to basically unsound conditions would give the financial structure a toppling blow. Philadelphia, the headquarters of Jay Cooke, felt the impact first. Banks and brokerage houses immediately began to announce suspension as runs started and customers demanded their deposits. The force of the blow became cumulative as it covered more and more territory.

Even now, the optimistic *Herald* still saw no reason for worry. On September 19th it said: "The country is too prosperous and wealthy to be seriously disturbed by the collapse of a few speculators or ephemeral banking institutions." But the trouble was more basic. Commodore Vanderbilt, partially retired and perfectly secure, had time to be analytical. Said he: "Building railroads from nowhere to nowhere at public expense is not a legitimate undertaking. Men are trying to do four times as much business as they should."

On the 19th Fisk & Hatch suspended, and the Fourth National Bank, their depository, followed. Thirty-five other banks and brokerage houses announced inability to meet their obligations the same day. How many more would have followed it is impossible to say. The Governors of the Stock Exchange took prompt action to avert a landslide and the temporary suspension of trading on the Stock Exchange halted the procession—but only for a short time.

According to Henry Clews this suspension of trading saved Jay Gould from disaster, as he was heavily involved. As a matter of fact, his broker, Charles J. Osborn, had sent in notice of suspension, but this arrived after the close of the Exchange and was not made public. The armistice gave Gould a chance to gather his forces and weather the storm.

On September 30th, after ten days' suspension, the Stock Exchange again opened its doors. But the trouble was not yet over, for the members convened only to listen to a long succession of additional failures. Stock prices, of course, had melted away. Savings banks were forced to demand sixty days' notice for withdrawal and President Grant's efforts to stem the tide by Government relief were unavailing. Until November this condition continued. The bubble of prosperity had burst and vanished. From the banks and brokerage houses the depression had spread to the Exchange, in that way had hurt the investing public and inevitably reached the industrial interests. Widespread unemployment added to the general distress. Gradually, however, as the subsequent deflation corrected the financial balance, the fury spent itself and the country began to resume the operation of its financial machinery. It took more than five years, however, for the country to recuperate completely, and only after dragging itself through this period of misfortune and misery did the ailing industrial and financial organs of the country at last completely resume their normal functions.

CHAPTER XI

JIM KEENE, CYRUS FIELD AND OTHERS

THE panic of 1873 numbered among its victims some of the great operators. Jay Cooke, whose failure was the immediate cause of the disturbance, was wiped out. Daniel Drew and Henry Smith were forced into bankruptcy and never came back. Younger men were coming up to fill the ranks, not only of those who went down in the struggle but those other figures who came close enough to disaster to give them warning of its proximity. Commodore Vanderbilt had practically retired, Daniel Drew was ruined, Jim Fisk was dead. Of all the leaders in the wars of the '60's only Jay Gould remained as an active figure, and his efforts were to be directed more and more to consolidations and mergers rather than to manipulative trading.

The newer leaders in the field were not of the same caliber. They were daring enough but in some way their activities lacked the sparkle and dramatic originality of the Erie pirates. They held the ground only for a short time, however, for soon were to come in the men, who by different methods of operation were to inaugurate an entirely new system of American enterprise. Between the Vanderbilt-Gould regime and the operations of the giants of the '90's was a group of men more interesting for their personalities than important for the accomplishments.

There was Charles F. Woerishoffer who was consistently a bear and who fought pool after pool with distressing persistence. He and James R. Keene were known for their extraordinary generosity. Although worth only about $5,000,000, Woerishoffer made presents of seats on the Stock Exchange to twenty brokers he favored. A seat was then worth about $25,000, so that on one day he gave away ten per cent of his fortune. His operations, as compared with his resources, were tremendous. Woerishoffer died in the midst of his career at the age of 43. Had he gone on it seems probable he would have failed entirely or amassed one of our large fortunes, so fearless were his operations and so consistently were they on a large scale.

James R. Keene was an Englishman who emigrated to California when he was seventeen. There he became a newspaper man for a time, then studied law and specialized in mining cases. As everbody did at the time he took a few flyers in mining stocks and was successful each time. A natural gambler Jim Keene decided that dealing in stocks was more exciting and profitable than the law. He did fairly well for a while, but his health failed and his physicians ordered a trip abroad. Before leaving California he had bought a few hundred shares of mining stock at an average of about $10 a share. After a year's absence Keene returned to find his stock worth over $200,000. He had been away during the great boom in mining stocks, and his trip had improved his finances even more than his health. Keene then reversed his position and sold short heavily, on the theory that the rise had been overdone. It turned out that he was right and his whirlwind operations netted him almost $3,000,000. Soon after that, encouraged by this series of successes, he decided to come to New York and match his wits with the Wall Street crowd. His success at first was amazing. By an unusual series of coups he ran his fortune up to $13,000,000. Jim Keene began to think that failure was impossible for him. His enjoyment of the situation was both intense and vociferous. The excitement of stock operations was not sufficient. Keene began to speculate in everything that came along —in wheat, lard, opium and fast horses. Out on the Pacific Coast he became an idol. One Western biographer wrote of him: "The California goose that was to be plucked wasn't plucked. Even Jay Gould, with all his shrewdness, gave it up as a bad job, and Vanderbilt condescends to confer with Keene on momentous occasions." But the goose eventually was plucked. There is no one more alert to spot a weak brother in the ranks than the Wall Street operator. Addison Cammack, a lesser figure on the Street, called on Jay Gould one day. He ventured the opinion that Keene was over-extending

himself. Keene's attempt at a grain corner was failing
and his position was very vulnerable. Gould told Cammack to go ahead and break Keene's stocks and he would
back him. The pressure was put on and Keene's embar-
rassment started. The banks began to call Keene's loans,
his brokers demanded more margin, his stocks began
to fall. First he sold out his tremendous holdings of wheat
at a great loss but this was not sufficient to avert failure.
The disaster was cumulative for the more stocks Keene
sold to protect the rest of his holdings the more did he
break his own market. It was not long before Cammack
was able to report to Gould that Jim Keene was back
to where he started. And as soon as Keene was wiped
out the barrage was lifted and the advance started. Had
Keene, three months later, held the same stocks which
caused his downfall, not only would he have had his
original capital but a profit of $10,000,000. On such
shifting bottoms are piled the sands of Wall Street success.

Another prominent figure in the higher circles of
Wall Street was Henry Villard. Villard like Woerishoffer
was a native of Germany. From 1879 to 1884 he was
probably the most active railroad operator in the Street.
Villard was originally a Washington newspaper cor-
respondent. In that capacity he made the acquaintance
of some influential politicians who were instrumental in
securing a railroad receivership for him. In this work he
secured some valuable experience. Villard showed great

HENRY VILLARD

The Northern Pacific proved too heavy a load
for him to carry.

ability in handling his first receivership and gained the confidence of many railroad men. His first large enterprise was in 1879. Two years before he had gone to Germany for a visit and upon his return determined to go into a venture on a large scale. He conceived the idea of purchasing the Oregon Steam Navigation Company and the Oregon Steamship Company and then combine them. The idea was a good one, but his entire capital then consisted of about $300,000 and the deal required several millions. He asked each company to give him a purchase option for a year for $100,000 which was done. Although the properties had not yet been acquired Villard at once organized a new corporation to consolidate the two old ones. He tried to interest Jay Gould in the scheme but was unsuccessful. An unusual personal charm was instrumental in inducing a Mr. Endicott and George Pullman to help him with the capital necessary to acquire the companies. The price of these companies was $3,500,000. Villard immediately went into action and soon after the new company was organized, securities to a par value of $12,000,000 were floated. Villard then instituted an aggressive publicity and market campaign which was successful in lifting the stock to 200. At this juncture another $9,000,000 in water was added. The public flotation of the stock proved simple and profitable. So successful was this operation that Villard was enabled to form a "blind pool" to acquire the Northern Pacific. Pullman, Endicott and Woerishoffer subscribed generously, and Villard was successful in securing control by open market purchases. Villard's methods were to bull a stock to inflated prices on the Exchange, and then balance it by new issues of stock. As soon as his stocks reached a figure high enough to discourage further public participation he split the stock and started a new rise. With very little capital Villard managed to swing tremendous railroad operations, and his success put him in a class just below the great manipulators. So delicately balanced were his operations, however, that the slightest disturbance might prove disastrous. His Northern Pacific deal put him in control for a time. Powerful interests, realizing his vulnerability, later forced him out of the road by an attack on Northern Pacific stock, and Henry Villard, discouraged by his reverses, retired with only a moderate fortune, spending his last days far away from Wall Street.

There have been very few men in Wall Street who also found distinction in other fields. Cyrus W. Field attained eminence as the man to lay the first Atlantic cable. His ambition for wealth drew him into the Street and there he met his downfall. Field was a man of the highest ideals, a quality which he soon found a great handicap in Wall Street affairs. He began his business life as a rag merchant and his rise in business and public life was steady, topped with the crowning event of his life, the successful construction of the Atlantic cable in

1866. He was not satisfied with that great feat, however. He wanted to surpass his brothers in accomplishment and was particularly anxious to become an industrial leader. One of his brothers sat on the United States Supreme Court bench, another was a leader of the New York bar and a third was a noted clergyman and editor. Field, particularly valuable to his associates because of the public esteem in which he was held, joined Russell Sage and Jay Gould in a combination organized for the purpose of securing control of the New York City elevated roads. The New York *Times* had said of this operation: "There is no more disgraceful chapter in the history of stock-jobbing than that which records the operations of Jay Gould, Russell Sage, Cyrus W. Field and their associates in securing control of the system of elevated railroads in New York City." Field felt keenly these uncushioned charges and he tried to change the methods used by his clique. The result of his efforts was only to antagonize Gould and Sage, who decided to get rid of the reformer in their ranks. They encouraged Field to go on buying, and in the meantime they sold all their stock. An aggressive bear campaign of unknown origin against the stock forced Cyrus Field into bankruptcy. Within a few weeks he was to lose his wife and see his son also a bankrupt. He had mastered the elements, but the wiles of Wall Street were too much for him. Cyrus Field's last days are graphically described by his daughter:

"It was at this time that disaster in business and calamities that were calculated to affect him far more keenly fell upon him, and what remained of his life was full of anguish, both mental and physical. On his seventy-second birthday he found that of the fortune that he had invested in the Atlantic cables, the elevated road and the Washington building, but £1,000 of Anglo-American stock remained, and had it not been for the kindness of his friend, Mr. J. Pierpont Morgan, he could not in May, 1892, have gone to his country home. It was Mr. Morgan also who advanced the necessary money to keep in force the premium on Mr. Field's life insurance policies. It was thought that the change to the country would benefit him but in fact it only increased his distress and his weakness. Early on the morning of July 12th his family was called, and watched by his side from half-past four until ten minutes before ten, when the rest he had so longed for was given."

Russell Sage remained a power in Wall Street to the end of his days. Born poor, his business life was so uniformly successful as to be almost colorless. By dint of keen business judgment, assisted by an unscrupulous nature, he acquired a large fortune. His activities in Wall Street were on a generous scale, but not particularly dramatic. Alert, resourceful and unscrupulous, he ran his fortune up to $20,000,000. His name is perpetuated in a great charitable foundation established by his widow, and it is by the Russell Sage Foundation that the world remembers him.

Of the others there are few worthy of mention. Only one more figure of the period before the great industrial consolidations need here be considered, and his importance lies not so much in his own operations, as in the fact that his partner was no less a personage than former President Ulysses S. Grant. The firm of Grant and Ward was for a time an important factor in Wall Street, and when it went down the fall not only shattered the life of the colorful General, but precipitated the financial panic of 1884.

II

Steadily rising stock prices had marked the five years of market activity previous to 1884. The market had finally shaken off the lethargy which followed the panic of 1873 and had bounded forward with renewed animation. Resumption of specie payment, ending the fluctuation in United States currency, had stimulated confidence and encouraged expansion. Crops were good, new railway building was resumed, credit was easy and the stage was set for a renewed and extensive revival.

In 1884 Jay Gould was still the dominant figure in the market, although his interests were now centered on consolidations, rather than on simon-pure speculative operations. By a skillful coup he had secured control of the Western Union Telegraph Company and had amalgamated it with his own American Union Telegraph Company. Together with Russell Sage and Cyrus Field he had successfully arranged a consolidation of the three competing New York elevated railways, the operation which finally broke Cyrus Field. Cornelius Vanderbilt's son, William H., had succeeded to his vast properties but made no effort to extend his holdings. Indeed he decided to reduce his properties by selling out his New York Central stock. Making his wishes known to Wall Street resulted in the formation of a syndicate to purchase the stock with a view to effecting a wide public distribution. After protracted negotiations a sale very favorable to the syndicate was effected. The price was $120 a share, then ten points below the market. The sale at so liberal a concession would seem to substantiate Vanderbilt's contention that he sold only because of the pressure of public opinion. "There is a certain feeling," said Vanderbilt, "among the public about one man having so much—I won't say it's wrong or that it's right, but there is such a feeling. I am a man who understands the public sentiment and I am always ready to meet it." This statement contrasts markedly with his earlier "The public be damned!" but it was undoubtedly sincere. In the transaction J. Pierpont Morgan, then a junior partner in Drexel, Morgan and Company, was the leading figure, and from this negotiation dates his rise to a dominant position in Wall Street affairs. Jay Gould made no concession to public opinion, for while William H. Vanderbilt was distributing a part of his enormous holdings Jay Gould was taking on new lines. Of the Central stock, he took at least 50,000 shares, and soon after he gained control of the Denver Pacific, Kansas Pacific and finally the Union Pacific. Gould manifested in the operation and consolidation of these roads a striking constructive ability. With the passing of Daniel Drew and Jim Fisk, and since his unpleasant encounter with the Erie reformers, Gould had abandoned his earlier and purely manipulative and pirating operations, and turned to constructive expansion, which was a more praiseworthy but none the less profitable endeavor.

In the few years just before the disaster of 1884 the market, just as before the panic of 1873, was staging a boom. Continually good news was released. Hardly a day passed without the report of a new railway consolidation, and the public, its previous wounds already forgotten, had again entered the Wall Street arena in force. By 1883 scattered warnings of an impending crash were noted, but, as usual, few paid any attention. In that year crops were poor and trade showed signs of slackening. The stock market was cushioning the coming of the big crash by a steady although not serious decline. One individual, whose persuasive abilities had been successful in enlisting former President Grant's active partnership in his schemes, was responsible for the final crash.

THE STORY OF WALL STREET

In the late '70's a young man named Ferdinand Ward came to be known as a rising figure in Wall Street. A youth of sound upbringing, the son of a minister, he came to the Street well recommended, and his steady rise seemed a just reward for his worthy efforts. Starting as a clerk on the Produce Exchange he entered into speculation in flour, and was fairly successful. He widened his field to trading in railroad securities and here his success was spectacular. Some one called him "the young Napoleon of Wall Street." He liked this title and encouraged its use, at the same time extending his operations in an effort to prove the name not inappropriate. Ferdinand Ward was a combination of ability, resourcefulness, optimism, unscrupulousness and bluff. His growing reputation made his cumulative success the easier, and General Grant's son, Ulysses jr., soon came under his influence. "Buck" Grant was then twenty-eight and rather slow-witted. His only accomplishment up to that time had been the successful wooing of a very rich man's daughter, and in looking around for a profitable, yet genteel occupation, young Grant naturally chose Wall Street. The firm of Grant & Ward was soon formed, and to "Buck" it meant getting $100,000 from his father-in-law, and then having a place in the business world and $3,000 a month drawing account. To Ferdinand Ward it meant the opportunity of getting close to General Grant and making good use of this valuable connection. It was not long before the General, led on by Ward's persuasiveness and apparent financial ability, had also invested $100,000, becoming a special partner in the firm.

Ward's method was a Ponzi scheme. Without a great deal of real constructive ability his plan was to attract capital from many different sources, pay large returns to his followers from their own capital, and thus give the impression of an affluent investment business. Into his net were drawn not only the Grants, but the president of the Marine National Bank, the venerable though gullible James D. Fish. The latter put his bank's resources at Ward's command. The connection was at first a regular banking relation, but under Ward's stimulus it gradually turned into a conspiracy to profit from irregular methods. The Grants sat in their comfortable offices, signed all papers that were handed to them and were entirely innocent of what was going on. Ward went so far as to get General Grant to sign a letter clearly indicating that the firm had valuable government contracts. This letter Ward used to get further investments in the firm from influential and wealthy individuals. After the explosion Grant said that he did not know what he was signing, as he trusted Ward implicitly and signed everything Ward asked him to. Young Ferdinand's infectious optimism held his investors, many of them millionaires, and the reassuring return of profits served to prevent any embarrassing inquiries. The endless chain could not continue forever, of course. A young man named Miller had once attempted the same scheme in Brooklyn and ended in jail. Ferdinand Ward's attempt was much more ambitious and his manipulations were on a grander scale. The inevitable crash was to have consequences proportionately disastrous.

In this chain, the Marine National Bank, of which Fish was president, first began to feel the strain. On Sunday, May 4, 1884, "the young Napoleon," now fast approaching his financial Waterloo, called on General Grant and told him the Marine Bank was in difficulties. Grant couldn't understand what that had to do with their firm and Ward explained. The difficulty was only temporary, of course, but Grant & Ward had large sums on deposit there. If $300,000 could be raised at once and placed in the Marine Bank, it would give the bank a chance to tide over, realize on some of its assets, and pull through, thus saving the firm's money. They needed the money only for one day, Ward told Grant. It would be returned on Tuesday, without fail.

Grant was then a sick man. He did not quite understand the reasoning but he trusted Ward implicitly, and he hobbled over to the house of William H. Vanderbilt to get the loan. Vanderbilt's reply was not reassuring. "I don't care anything about the Marine National Bank," he said. "It can fail without disturbing me; and as for Grant & Ward—what I've heard about that firm would not justify me in lending it a dime.

But I'll give you $150,000 personally." He wrote out the check. "To you—to General Grant—I'm making this loan, and not to the firm." The circumstances of the loan were humiliating, but Grant meekly accepted, and hurried to turn the check over to Ward.

In the meantime Ward had been to see Jay Gould and many others, but apparently they all knew more about the firm than did Grant, and not a nickel was he able to raise. Ward then did a characteristic thing. He pocketed Vanderbilt's check, cashed it for his personal use, and never made the deposit in the Marine Bank.

On May 7, 1884, the Marine National Bank closed its doors. The announcement stated that the failure had been due to overdrafts by Grant & Ward, in spite of the fact that the firm's books showed a balance of $600,-000 to the credit of the firm. As a matter of fact, Ward had overdrawn the account more than $2,000,000 but the books had been juggled to hide the situation. Even now, Ward reassured Grant that everything was all right, and Grant still believed him. But the next few days were to bare the tragic facts. Grant was not only ruined financially, but the great reputation he had acquired was now in danger of being destroyed. Thousands had lost by the swindle, and this fact Grant felt more than the loss of his own money.

For Grant it was the shattering blow. His part in the swindle had been devoid of any guilt. All he had ever gotten out of the firm had been his living expenses, al-

though his actual cash investment had been over $100,-
000. The value of his share on the books of the firm at
the time of the crash was $2,400,000. "I have made it
the rule of my life," he said, "to trust a man long after
other people gave him up; but I don't see how I can
trust any human being again." For James Fish the disaster meant seven years and for Ferdinand Ward ten
years in jail; for Ulysses Grant, it meant shattered hopes,
broken health, extreme poverty and an embittered attitude for the one remaining year of his colorful life.

The firm's liabilities amounted to more than $16,-
000,000; its assets were $67,000. This in spite of the
fact that its books showed assets of $27,000,000. The
failure on so large a scale shook the machinery of Wall
Street and was the immediate cause of a financial panic.
Had conditions been more stable the Street could have
weathered the storm without any serious results, but a
gradual decline in general business conditions found
many firms and individuals vulnerable, and this last
blow shattered the feeble resistance.

III

The suspensions of the Marine National Bank and
the firm of Grant & Ward came right on top of Henry
Villard's failure in January, 1884, and his withdrawal
from Wall Street. On May 13th the Street had another
shock. It was discovered that John C. Eno, president

of the Second National Bank, had robbed it of almost $4,000,000. The market broke again on May 14th, and George I. Seney, a leading figure and president of the Metropolitan Bank and several railroads, went under in the crash. Stocks had little support, and the shorts brought up their heaviest ammunition. In a few weeks New York Central broke twenty-eight points, Western Union twenty-six, Delaware, Lackawanna & Western thirty-four and the rest of the list proportionately. Money went to 150 per cent and some of the leading brokerage houses could not carry their stocks. Even the firm of the president of the New York Stock Exchange, Fisk and Hatch, suspended payment. Russell Sage was temporarily embarrassed but weathered the storm. He had been selling puts freely and the landslide placed him in an unenviable position. For a few days he refused payment on his contracts but soon resumed, disbursing $7,000,000 in three days. Four banks suspended, and even Jay Gould was rumored to be in difficulties. To effectively squelch these persistent reports, the latter called in Cyrus W. Field, Russell Sage and Frank Work, and displayed unhypothecated securities to the value of $53,000,000. Gould offered further to show $20,000,000 in bonds. This dramatic exhibition rallied the market but only temporarily.

For the rest of the year stock prices declined as public confidence waned. The panic, however, was confined to financial circles, and did not affect industrial conditions.

The fortunate occurrence of a record corn crop early in 1885 was a boon to the railroads and the tide gradually turned. Not, however, before several other banks and brokerage houses closed their doors. On Jan. 15, 1885, the prominent firm of J. J. Cisco and Company suspended payment, causing a fresh drop. Their suspension was due to the sudden calling in by Hetty Green of $25,000,000 in securities and $475,000 in cash from this firm. This payment she insisted upon in full at once, regardless of the fact that her husband owed the same firm $800,000 at the time. Inability to respond to her call forced the Cisco firm into bankruptcy.

About this time J. Pierpont Morgan, encouraged by his success in the distribution of Vanderbilt's stock, took a leading position. At his suggestion, and because of his masterly negotiations, the Pennsylvania Railroad, the New York Central and the West Shore Railroad were induced to stop their rate-cutting war and enter into a truce. Mr. Morgan's first great achievement as a harmonizer caused an immediate rise in the securities of all these railroads and ended the persistent general decline. This arrangement was the signal for a fresh bull movement, which soon wiped out the effects of the Grant & Ward panic and started a new rise, at the same time bringing to the fore an entirely new group of men, radically different in their methods and procedure from the manipulators associated with the first railroad expansion.

The next period was to see also an entirely new movement come into being. Up to the early '90's the railroads were the chief center of interest for Wall Street. Mining and oil stocks were heavily traded in, but the new trust movement shifted the emphasis to the industrials, which up to that time had been considered of so little importance as to be traded in only in the unlisted department of the Stock Exchange. To the honorary titles of "railroad magnates," held by such men as Vanderbilt and Gould, were to be added the new distinctions of "oil barons," "steel kings," "coal magnates," and "captains of industry." An ever widening public interested in things financial was to accord these honors to men like James J. Hill and E. H. Harriman in railway consolidation, John D. Rockefeller, Henry H. Rogers, Charles Pratt and H. M. Flagler in oil development, Andrew Carnegie, H. C. Frick and Charles M. Schwab in the steel industry, and J. P. Morgan and Jacob H. Schiff in banking and finance. More and more, bankers were to have a hand, and often the final word, in the tremendous ventures in formation. And more and more the important figures in Wall Street were to be those men whose abilities were constructive rather than manipulative. The country was ripe for the beginning of the stupendous trust movement.

CHAPTER XII

THE EVOLUTION OF "BIG BUSINESS"

PRIOR to 1865 railroads and manufacturing establishments had been mainly local organizations. A length of a few hundred miles was regarded as best adapted for efficient railway management and only one road exceeded one thousand miles. The tracks of the roads in existence were of varied widths, so that it usually was impossible to run cars of one road over the lines of a connecting road. In the same way manufacturing organizations did not have any of the advantages of large-scale management. After 1865 the tendency was towards the consolidation of these smaller units into larger ones. The high protective tariff was encouraging to expansion and this trend continued steadily. With this movement the corporate form of organization came to be used widely in the United States, replacing the partnerships of the previous period. In this development leaders were divided between men of constructive attitudes, like Vanderbilt, and the manipulators, headed by men like Drew and Gould. The formation of large railway lines did not decrease the competition between the roads. For, where before there were hundreds of small roads struggling for existence, there was now a comparatively small number of large roads battling for monopoly. Discriminations, rate wars and rebates became the common practice. The formation of the Interstate Commerce Commission in 1887 was the first important step of the Government towards supervision of the varied activities of the railroads, and a forerunner of still more stringent legislation. The consolidation movement of the railroads was not halted, however, and by 1900 more than half of the mileage of the United States was controlled by six powerful groups. The Vanderbilt, Morgan, Harriman and Pennsylvania groups each owned mileage of approximately 20,000, the Gould group 16,000, and the Hill group 5,000.

In the industrial field, the combination movement developed more slowly, but gained great impetus in the late '80's. Directed up to that time mainly for purposes of efficiency, the promoters of the enterprises soon saw the possibility of using these combinations to stifle outside competition and create a limited monopoly. Stronger competitors in an industry first co-operated in fixing standard prices, limiting output, and determining exclusive territory. These practices gradually resulted in the formation of pools by the competing interests, designed to serve as a means of carrying out the provisions of secret agreements, and finally in the formation of trusts. This tendency was soon noted by the public, and aroused a fear, not without basis, that these huge organizations, ever widening in influence and growing in power, might actually control the necessities of life. As early as 1884 an organized Anti-Monopoly party appeared in the national political campaign. By 1890 fifteen States had adopted legislation to prevent conspiracies or agreements in restraint of free competition. By that time every State in the Union except New Jersey, Delaware and West Virginia had enacted similar legislation. Corporations chartered in these States escaped the effects of this legislation however, and their coffers were filled with the fees from the new organizations. Congress tried to put a stop to this practice by the enactment of the Sherman Anti-Trust Act on July 2, 1890. This statute was drafted in response to a public demand, but so anxious was Congress to satisfy the voters, that the law was rushed through, drafted hastily and in such general terms, that not for ten years could its provisions be enforced. Between 1860 and 1890, twenty-four combinations had been organized with a nominal capital of $436,000,000. In the next ten years, 157 new combinations were formed with a total nominal capital of $3,150,000,000. In 1901 this movement was topped by the super-consolidation—the United States Steel Corporation, a combination of combinations, capitalized at more than one billion dollars.

In the banking field, the same tendency of centralization and consolidation was evident. By 1900, the Rocke-

WALL STREET IN THE NINETIES

feller, the Kuhn-Loeb and the Morgan interests dominated banking to such an extent that it was doubtful if any great business enterprise could have been started without the aid of one of these groups.

II

The consolidation movement, which spread to the industrials late in the 1880's, soon began to grow faster than sound expansion warranted. Along with these consolidations, most of which were logical in plan, conservative in scope and efficient in results, there came into being scores of organizations floated by outside promoters. Many of these started with such top-heavy capitalization, most of it watered stock, that there was little chance of success. The apparent success of some of these combinations and the rapid rise in their stock, induced a receptive attitude in the investing public's mind, and made it easy for promoters to market large quantities of valueless stock.

The National Cordage Company flotation is a typical case in point. It had been organized in 1890 with the intention of controlling the twine industry. It took in most of the existing twine concerns, using coercion where necessary. To one large manufacturer who refused to enter the combine, it agreed to pay $200,000 a year to shut down his plant and keep out of business. Originally incorporated with $10,000,000 in common stock, it soon increased this to $20,000,000. The management headed by James M. Waterbury, was composed of men more conversant with the gyrations of the ticker than the manufacture of twine. For about two years it paid large dividends, although unwarranted by earnings. Its stock had been widely distributed and it was a favorite for small traders on the Stock Exchange. It was headed for disaster and the slightest disturbance would bring it to a certain fall. This came with the stringency of 1893 and the first signs of coming distress found Cordage common stock plunging down from the artificial level of $75 a share to $15. Even that point was difficult to maintain and less than four years after its organization National Cordage went into a receiver's hands, a total loss to the common stockholders.

The panic of 1893 was caused by the combination of an unsound inflation of money policy by the government and an extraordinary overcapitalization of new combinations as the result of the trust movement. Finally toppling the structure was an unusual overspeculation on the part of the public, infected by the tremendous activity in industrial consolidations.

In 1890 the Sherman Silver Purchase Act was put in operation. It called for the rapid redemption of silver currency in circulation with a consequent depletion of the government's gold reserve. This condition was later stopped but not until the country's credit had been seriously impaired and great quantities of gold had been exported.

At the same time many overcapitalized combinations, floated by optimistic promoters who immediately declared large dividends as an aid to market distribution and manipulation, found themselves in difficulties. Many of these outside promoters had paid exorbitant prices for constituent companies, their only interest being the rapid completion of their consolidation plan. The promoters had no permanent interest in these huge companies, since they disposed of their stock as soon as possible at inflated prices. The result of such a condition was that the companies soon found themselves unable to meet the high dividend rates already established. They also discovered that it is one thing to buy up all their competitors and another thing to keep new ones from entering into the business.

The Stock Exchange began to reflect these inflated conditions early in 1893 although the effect throughout the country was not felt for six months. Call money went to fifty per cent, and by May, 1893, liquidation became urgent. A stringent condition in Australia forced English investors to sell American stocks to protect their interests there and this added to the wave of selling. It was just this time that the National Cordage Company selected to announce a new issue of $2,500,000 in preferred stock. It resulted not in new subscription but in wholesale selling of this "weak sister's" stocks.

The Cordage rout sent three brokers to the wall. The company could not raise a $50,000 loan to meet the payroll, and receivers were appointed. From that point the landslide gathered force. S. V. White, one of the largest Street speculators and promoter of the Whiskey Trust, went to the wall in an attempt to protect his holdings. Two of his brokers went down with him. Call loan rates, for some mysterious reason, now relaxed, and the market remained firm for a time. But this was only temporary. On May 9th, three banks failed in Chicago and one in New York. Charles Foster, Secretary of the Treasury under Harrison (and while in office chief advocate of the Silver Purchase Act which was largely blamed for the stringency), was now the head of the banking firm of Foster & Co. By a fatal coincidence his firm was one of the first to feel the force of the blow and all the firms and banks he was connected with failed. His prominence shattered what little public confidence there was left and the decline turned into a rout. Hundreds of banks, mainly in the Middle West, went under and the weakness spread to the grain market. By the 29th of May call money had shot up to seventy-five per cent. Throughout June and July conditions became worse and even the large New York banks refused to pay gold against checks. Even currency went to a premium value against checks and savings banks were forced to demand advance notice from depositors wishing to withdraw funds. The crisis spread to the railroads and both the Northern and Union Pacific went into bankruptcy.

The repeal of the Silver Purchase Act came as a welcome relief to the business world, and President Cleveland's heroic financial measures gradually restored the semblance of order. In 1893 there were 642 bank failures and more than 15,000 large commercial failures. About 30,000 miles of railroad went into bankruptcy. President Cleveland entered into an arrangement with J. Pierpont Morgan and August Belmont, the latter representing the Rothschilds, to sell them about $62,000,-000 in thirty-year bonds for gold at 104½. The fact that the Morgan-Belmont syndicate resold the issue at 112¼ caused much public comment and dissatisfaction. But an important condition was that more than half of the gold used for payment must come from abroad. The Treasury reserve was down to $40,000,000, and the Government needed gold badly to replenish the exhaustion consequent upon the silver purchase policy.

Throughout 1894, 1895, and into 1896, there was continued weakness incident to the country's slow convalescence. Not until 1896 was the Government able to replenish fully its gold reserves, and only with McKinley's election was business confidence fully restored. The passing of the free silver agitation fostered by the fiery William Jennings Bryan dispersed the last cloud that hung over the business horizon and led to the famous McKinley stock market boom. The Spanish-

American War was also a great factor in the return of business prosperity. The bull market, which started with McKinley's election in 1896, continued at a great pace until another period of trust expansion and public over-speculation ended in the disaster of 1903.

CHAPTER XIII

ROCKEFELLER AND OIL

L IKE all other great American industries, the oil business had its small beginnings, its day of romance, its period of consolidation and regular routine. In the early 1840's, "rock oil," as it was then called, had been found in various parts of Pennsylvania, Kentucky, Ohio, and the section now part of West Virginia. Farmers in these regions found it on the surface of streams and creeks, and sometimes in wells driven to tap supplies of brine for the manufacture of salt. The brine was then considered the valuable part drawn from the wells, and the "rock oil" was often drawn off as an impurity and discarded. About 1845, some enterprising young men conceived the idea of selling oil as a medicine, and a company was organized to market oil as an excellent tonic for "cholera morbus, liver complaint, bronchitis, and consumption." One of the group who formed this business, Samuel Kier, discovered by chance that his medicine could be used as a lubricant and luminant. After having a sample analyzed by a chemist, he commenced to refine crude oil by the process of distillation on a small scale. About 1849, S. H. Bissell, a young journalist, saw one of Kier's advertisements, and bought some of the oil for the purpose of analyzing it. He went to Professor Silliman of Yale, who confirmed the value of oil for lighting and lubrication. Bissell immediately started an active campaign to secure backing for a company to be organized to commercialize oil on a large scale. By 1854, he had been successful in enlisting the support of some wealthy men, and at once began to hunt for oil in large quantities. Up to that time, only the oil that had come to the surface by accident, had been used, and no effort had ever been made to sink wells for the sole purpose of extracting oil from the earth. A former railway conductor by the name of Edwin Drake was sent by Bissell and his associates to the western part of Pennsylvania to sink wells. Land was leased at low prices, and for several years, Drake persisted in his efforts, to the amused pity of the local wise men. In August, 1859, Drake finally struck oil at Titusville, Pennsylvania, and one of America's greatest industries was launched.

The news of Drake's strike spread fast. Farmers in the section at once began to experiment on their own lands, with astounding success. The land for miles around was soon dotted with oil wells, and the farmers in the section soon found themselves wealthy men. The same soil with which they had struggled for years for a bare subsistence, now belched forth thousands of barrels of oil each day. From Western Pennsylvania, the news spread to West Virginia and the Allegheny River Valley, and these sections rivalled Titusville in their sudden rise to prominence and wealth. A country doctor, who gave up pills for oil, drew a fortune of $1,-500,000 from a single well. Prospectors, investors, working men, confidence men, speculators, gamblers, and women of easy virtue rushed into the enchanted kingdom. Towns sprang up like magic. Everything for miles around was splashed with oil, and all the countryside was dotted with derricks. It took only a few thousand dollars to drill a well, and a gusher might yield a million dollars—or nothing. Fashionable New York hotels were soon filled with a new tribe of "oil millionaires," who feverishly began to accumulate town houses, bank accounts, stocks and bonds—and culture.

To many this new discovery meant fortune and position; to others it meant only fragmentary hopes, shattered by lack of luck in striking exactly the right spot. To an enterprising young commission merchant in Cleveland, John D. Rockefeller by name, it meant a new economic force released into the world of business enterprise, a force the importance of which he was quick to realize and determined to control.

When Edwin Drake struck oil in Titusville, Rockefeller was twenty. Born in Richford, New York, in 1839, he was taken by his father to a farming community in upper Ohio, where he received the bare rudiments of a formal education. At the age of sixteen he was already at work as a clerk at $12.50 a month. Aided by his father, now prospering as a travelling quack doctor, he had entered the produce commission business in Cleveland with one Maurice Clark, after an apprentice-ship as a bookkeeper in a similar firm. Their business prospered from the very beginning, and all during the Civil War the future oil king remained at his desk adding to his tiny fortune as the price of commodities soared with the demands of the government.

By 1861, Rockefeller was in Titusville, the center of the oil region of Northwestern Pennsylvania, looking over the possibilities. Both Clark and he decided that the most money, with the least risk, was to be made in the refining, rather than in the producing end of the new industry, and the two young merchants joined in erecting a refinery in Cleveland. As technical expert, they employed Samuel Andrews. At the same time they cautiously continued operating their profitable produce business. By 1865, in less than four years of operation, almost $100,000 had been drawn from profits from the refinery by the partners, so immediately remunerative was the venture. The possibilities piqued Rockefeller's cupidity, and he resolved upon an extension of his in-terests. Rockefeller realized the future of the refining business better than Clark and proposed to Clark that the latter give Rockefeller his share in the refinery in exchange for Rockefeller's interest in the produce busi-ness. Clark agreed, and Rockefeller became sole owner.

JOHN D. ROCKEFELLER

"Sane in every respect save one, he is money mad."
—Mark Hanna, an intimate friend.

John D. realized that competition would become keener as the industry became stabilized, and that it was necessary to get a large capital fund to secure a rapid extension before the establishment of too many competitors. He therefore approached Henry M. Flagler, a man whose ability and ingenuity were on a par with Rockefeller's. Besides being able to supply the young business with a moderate amount of new capital, Flagler's value was great also in his excellent connections with wealthy men in Cleveland, and his ability to interest them in his ventures. The richest man in Cleveland then was Stephen Harkness, and Flagler was successful in securing his financial backing. In the meantime, Andrews had proved himself extremely valuable as a technical man, and was given a partnership interest. The new firm was called Rockefeller, Andrews and Flagler, Harkness preferring a silent connection for the present. Cleveland, in spite of its distance from the oil fields, was already an important refining center. In this district Rockefeller's firm soon became the second largest refinery. Flagler was the man who first conceived the idea of buying up some of the smaller competing refineries in Cleveland, and started the plan by getting a small competitor who wasn't making a profit for $4,700. The acquisition of the competing refinery proved to be a successful venture, and Flagler and John D. began to discuss the possibilities of extending this method on a large scale. The two oil men lived in adjoining houses, and spent almost all their time together. Their mutual business interests accorded with a perfect personal understanding, and in their walks to the refinery each day, they often discussed their extension plans, in complete agreement that the situation promised success. Several other small refineries in Cleveland were brought in, and this method of extinguishing competition proved feasible. The reputation of the firm grew as unit after unit was brought under its control, and the partners began to consider spreading their business into other oil districts.

The germ of the desire for complete monopoly started with Flagler's attempt to secure special rebates from the railroads. By 1868, the oil-carrying trade had become an important source of revenues for the Pennsylvania, the New York Central, the Erie, and the Lake Shore Railroads. By representation of great power over other large refineries, Flagler induced the Lake Shore to give his firm a special rate of $1.75 a barrel as against the usual charge of $2.40 a barrel, in consideration of the firm giving the Lake Shore their exclusive business and using their influence to divert to them the business of other refineries. This rebate enabled Rockefeller, Andrews and Flagler to undersell their competitors. Their increased business soon made them the largest refinery in Cleveland, and the success of this scheme induced more ambitious plans. Meanwhile, the firm had continued the policy of buying up smaller rival plants, scrapping the hopeless ones and reorganizing the others under Andrews's efficient management. Of Cleveland's refinery capacity of 11,000 barrels a day, the enterprising group in 1869 controlled 1,500 barrels.

On January 10, 1870, in anticipation of national expansion, the Standard Oil Company of Cleveland was organized with a capital stock of $1,000,000, the original incorporators being John D. Rockefeller, Samuel Andrews, Henry M. Flagler, Stephen V. Harkness and William Rockefeller, John D.'s brother. When the company was organized it had already attained the rank of the largest individual refiner in the United States, and the ground was prepared for still further extension of interests and power. The success of the early rebate arrangement with the Lake Shore Railroad seemed a good reason for making a general and even more advantageous arrangement with all the oil-carrying roads. Together with some large Philadelphia and Pittsburgh refineries, the Standard Oil Company organized the Southern Improvement Company, which entered into a secret rate arrangement with the New York Central, the Erie and the Pennsylvania Railroads. The agreement called for the fixing of a public rate of $2.56 a barrel from the oil regions in Pennsylvania to New York, and eighty cents the barrel from the oil regions to Cleveland. The Southern Improvement Company, controlled by the Standard Oil and three other large refineries, was to receive a rebate of $1.06 on all oil shipped to New York, and forty cents on oil sent to Cleveland. Not only were these amounts to be paid to the Southern Improvement Company for oil shipped by these refineries, but also on oil shipped by competitors, who were to pay the regular full rate. The toll which the independents would have to pay would fatally cripple their business. Knowledge of this arrangement soon became public, and so furiously was it attacked that it was abandoned in response to a concerted offensive by the public, press, and independent oil refiners. But not before the Standard Oil had been able to buy up twenty-one of the twenty-six competing refineries in Cleveland crippled by this arrangement, in exchange for cash or Standard Oil stock. In spite of the continued success of the Standard, cash was not very plentiful in its coffers, due to steady expansion, and every effort was made to get the competitors to accept stock. Those who were weak enough to be persuaded became very rich men. The expansion of the Standard was paid for almost entirely out of profits, and as a result, so stringent was their cash position at times, that it was necessary to pay for current purchases in company stock, a plan that was resorted to whenever acceptable to the creditor.

In 1872, when the railroads and the Standard Oil finally abandoned the rebate system, at least temporarily, Rockefeller was thirty-three. About this time, he became acquainted with John D. Archbold, then a small oil producer, and induced him to join the Standard forces. William H. Vanderbilt had also become a large stockholder, and his New York Central road gave the Standard special rates for its freight. About the same time, Jay Gould, acting for the Erie, turned over its Weehawken terminal to the Standard in return for a guaranty of fifty per cent of its freight. More quietly than in the abortive plan of the Southern Improvement, Rockefeller and Flagler had succeeded in instituting again the discriminatory rates, this time without the aid of any other refining companies. They had also formed an organization called the Central Association, taking in the two largest competing refineries, which was to act in co-operative price setting, with the ultimate idea of a general combination. As early as 1874, these two master negotiators had been successful in getting Charles Pratt and H. H. Rogers, the owners of Charles Pratt and Company, the largest refinery in New York, to sell out in exchange for Standard Oil stock, their refinery to be operated, however, as an apparent competitor.

John D. Rockefeller and his associates were the first group in the United States to develop the idea of a combination effectively disposing of competition. Before the organization of the Standard Oil Company, none of the consolidations and combinations in the United States had been on a national scale, nor had they used any coercion to restrict competition. Those in existence had been confined almost entirely to railways, as industrial and manufacturing establishments were not yet national enterprises. The largest of them up to that date had been Cornelius Vanderbilt's New York Central lines, made up of the formerly competing Harlem, Hudson, and old New York Central roads.

The ambitions of Rockefeller, Flagler, Pratt, and the rest of the famous Standard Oil group, step by step, as new methods were devised, and new weapons discovered, urged them on to what in time amounted to a virtual monopoly of the oil industry in the world. Ida M. Tarbell has contributed to this story her brilliant *History of the Standard Oil Company,* which gives an accurate and exhaustive account of the methods of the group, and the development of its interests. Very recently, John K. Winkler has given us a sprightly account of Rockefeller's personal habits in his *John D.— A Portrait in Oils.* Around the legendary figure of this great organizer have sprung up many legends. Once, probably sharing with Jay Gould the doubtful distinction of being the most hated man in America, he has come, as the result of the diplomacy of his son, and his huge philanthropies—his benefactions have already reached the stupendous figure of $700,000,000—to be held as one of the revered men of the generation. As late as 1907, Judge Kenesaw Landis echoed public opinion when he made this pronouncement, preliminary to imposing his famous $29,240,000 fine: "You wound society more deeply than does he who counterfeits the coin or steals letters from the mail." On July 8, 1929, on the ninetieth birthday of John D. Rockefeller, not a newspaper of general circulation had anything but praise for the venerable billionaire.

It cannot be said that Rockefeller, in his campaign of acquisition, acted in any way unfairly towards the refineries he acquired or combined with. He openly welcomed all refineries into the Central Association, providing they were willing to lease their plants to the Standard. For those who did, he secured the same special rates from the railroads that the Standard enjoyed. They all profited, and only the stubborn outsiders and the public felt any loss. The gradual centralization bore fruit in a steady rise in the price of oil, with no increase in production or refining costs, a condition which geometrically increased the Standard Oil Company's profits.

That pressure and intimidation were used to force independents to join the Central Association, is clearly evident. For brutal tactics, neither Rockefeller nor Flagler were suited by temperament, and John D. Archbold conducted this end of the campaign. Simultaneously with the combination of refineries, the Standard was fast acquiring a large proportion of the pipe lines and special tank cars in the country.

By 1884, according to Ida Tarbell, the oil regions looked upon John D. Rockefeller "with superstitious awe." In 1882, he had moved his headquarters to New

York, and it seemed to him only a matter of a short time before there would be a complete monopoly. There had been several legislative and Congressional investigations, but the results of these inquiries had been nil, and the Standard was pressing on remorselessly in its campaign of acquisition. It had spread its trade over all the world, and had blessed the furthermost regions with the miracle of artificial light. Over eighty-five per cent of the oil industry was controlled absolutely by the Standard, and the press and public were becoming fully aroused to the dangerous possibilities of the situation. Aroused, but powerless. Not until Theodore Roosevelt brought the force of his "trust-busting" campaign against the Standard, were its plans ever halted.

Of John D. Rockefeller's personal life and motives, not much is known. Of his genuine piousness, his natural gentleness, and his unselfish generosity, there can be no question. Rockefeller's questionable tactics in amassing his power and great fortune may have been due to the fact that Rockefeller probably never saw these conditions in their proper perspective, so obsessed was he with the desire for money. When he was a young man, he is said to have exclaimed, "I'm bound to be rich." He himself is quoted as having said: "Most pioneers who have changed the established order have been misunderstood and cruelly persecuted." That he was not an egoist, we can judge from this estimate of his wife: "She was a woman of great sagacity. Without her keen advice, I should be a poor man." Perhaps Mark Hanna, intimately associated with Rockefeller from boyhood until Hanna's death, was right when he said of Rockefeller: "Sane in every respect save one—he is money mad."

John D. Rockefeller, now in his ninety-first year, occupies his time mainly in writing his autobiography. When that appears, perhaps we shall have a better understanding of this inconsistent genius, kind, gentle, and affectionate in all his personal relations—cruel, remorseless, and tyrannical in his business life.

CHAPTER XIV

HILL AND HARRIMAN

INTO the exclusive company of the business peerage of the United States two new railroad barons had won their way by the beginning of the twentieth century. In antecedents, early environment and training and business methods, James J. Hill, the railroad peer of the Northwest, and Edward H. Harriman, the broker-baron of the East, were widely separated.

Hill was born on September 16, 1838. Like many of the men whose achievements won them a prominent place in the business annals of America, Hill was of Irish-Scotch descent. His father was a fairly prosperous Canadian farmer, and until he died in 1852, was able to afford his son a good schooling. A naturally adventurous spirit led to the acceptance by young Hill of an invitation to visit one of his schoolmates in the Far West. At St. Paul, Minn., he missed connections, and instead of waiting several weeks for a packet or returning to his home, he decided to find a job. In this he was successful, and at the age of eighteen he became a shipping clerk for a Mississippi River steamship agent. In 1856 St.

HILL AND HARRIMAN

Paul was a small trading post of 5,000 inhabitants. Hill had found the section agreeable and his work pleasant and decided to settle in Minnesota. For the next six years he worked as a clerk with different shipping firms and decided to make this his business. The entire Minnesota territory could boast of only 150,000 population, but it was rapidly becoming a flour-milling center, and the development gave Hill an excellent opportunity to expand with the environment. By nature studious, the boy specialized in steamboat construction and methods of transportation, and the increasing opportunities of this growing territory found him well prepared. The Civil War, for Hill, as well as for almost every one of the eminently successful men with whom this story deals, meant additional commercial opportunity. By 1865 young Hill was in the forwarding and transportation business on his own account and started his career of accumulation. He soon began to appropriate a large share of the forwarding business in St. Paul, and became exclusive agent for two large packet companies. His growing importance in the business community can be noticed from some of the current items in the local newspapers. Although most of these were probably inspired by the enterprising young shipping agent, they serve nevertheless to indicate his activity and rapid advance. About 1866, we find this item: "James J. Hill has secured the contract for furnishing the Government with 15,000 bushels of oats at 58 cents a bushel.

As we have remarked before, Jim Hill has a habit of securing things when he goes after them." Shortly afterwards, the friendly editor carried this notice: "J. J. Hill is now prepared to give shippers the lowest rates ever quoted from here to Eastern points. Mr. Hill has nearly all the important carriers of freight on his own hands. He at first secured the agency of the Duluth Packet lines of river steamers. Then one by one, he has had the Chicago & Northwestern, the Milwaukee & Prairie du Chien, and the Illinois Central Railroad agencies placed under his control at this point."

The shipping business was very profitable for Hill, but its seasonal nature led him into adding a general commission business. The type of business he conducted was varied in nature. The Sears-Roebuck catalog scarcely ever recorded a more varied assortment than an order he received from a clergyman customer. It called for "two cases of gin, one case sugar, two tuning forks, and one copy each of the works of Tennyson and Longfellow," and was in due course filled to the complete satisfaction of the clergyman of catholic taste. Hill's business was constantly growing and the ingenious young *entrepreneur* lost no opportunity to increase his income in allied fields. Witness this news item: "Navigation having closed and the steamboat business having thus wound up, J. J. Hill has, with a spirit of enterprise which is commendable, converted

JAMES J. HILL

*He bought two streaks of rust and a right of way, and developed
a great railway system in the Northwest.*

his immense warehouse into a mammoth hay pressing establishment. If he cannot handle freight, he can press hay."

From this point, Hill's business development was rapid. Soon after he was married in 1867 he formed a short-lived partnership with a firm in Dubuque. His idea was to expand the territory of his business, but the new arrangement did not work out well. After its dissolution, he formed the firm of Hill, Griggs and Company, organized to do a general commission business in wood and coal. Able and aggressive, Hill was successful in securing the contract to furnish fuel to the St. Paul and Pacific Railroad Company. By 1875 he had bought out Griggs's interest and reorganized the firm into the Northwestern Fuel Company. Hill's increasing contact with railroads convinced him that in this form of transportation lay the greatest possibilities for development. He was now almost forty and worth not even $100,000. Dissatisfied with his comparatively slow financial progress, Hill gave up all his other interests in 1878, and set up as a shipping agent for railroads exclusively. About this time he definitely settled in the Northwest and, politically ambitious, became a naturalized American citizen.

From being a large shipping agent it was for Hill a natural step to enter the transportation business on his own account. Together with Norman W. Kittson, Hill started a line to Winnipeg. It carried both passengers and freight and consisted of a short railway line, a stage connection and a steamer. His business carried him to Winnipeg often, and there he met Donald A. Smith, then resident manager for the Hudson Bay Company and later Lord Strathcona, the railroad king of Canada. They were immediately impressed with each other, and a relationship started which was to develop into an intimate business connection in the building of the Canadian Pacific.

Smith, Hill and Kittson were three enterprising promoters, but there was little capital among them. Their determination to get rich quickly and their venturesome spirit led them into a very risky enterprise. Hill, particularly, was getting impatient. He was then almost forty-five and still not a very wealthy man. He decided to take a chance with a large railroad and the panic of 1873 gave him his opportunity. The St. Paul and Pacific Railroad, poorly managed, badly financed and dwarfed by the competing Northern Pacific, went under at the first signs of strain. When J. P. Farley was appointed receiver, he reported that this line was so run down, that only hand cars could be run over the rails. "Two streaks of rust and a right of way," some one described the road. The majority of its bonds were held by Dutch bankers, and their American agents held out little hope for any recovery. It was this road that Hill and his associates decided to buy. Unfortunately, even the bargain price for which it was on the market represented a great deal more money than the group could raise. The foreign bondholders were willing to sell very cheaply but for cash. Smith sent a friend to London to try to raise funds, promising him a share in the road, if successful. The optimistic friend reported progress, and the group made a firm offer on the basis of this assurance. After the papers for the purchase of the road were signed the London envoy reported failure and the cash was not forthcoming. The Dutch group knew of no one else who wanted the road at any price, and they finally consented to let Hill and his friends have the road on credit, accepting bonds and stock of the new company against a part of the purchase price. Without capital, but with a thorough knowledge of this section of the country and its needs, these men set to making a profitable property of this decrepit road. Their success was beyond even their wildest hopes.

Hill's methods then, as later in his larger development, were entirely constructive. Reared on the frontier, he knew its people and its potentialities. Unlike the speculative owner he took a long view of things. He employed publicity men to travel over the Eastern and Middle States and encourage emigration to the Northwest. He organized free excursions for prospective settlers. He did not wait for the Westward movement to gain momentum; he directed its rapid acceleration. Nor did he stop there. He helped build towns, supervised production, and instituted credit facilities for his settlers. Along the lines of his railways he saw virgin prairies spring into prosperous farms and thriving towns. The force of Hill's campaign to settle the country reached out to foreign countries, and from the northern countries of Europe a new group of Vikings sailed forth to America. Into the upper Mississippi country came almost one-third of Denmark's population, and a great exodus from Sweden and Norway helped to swell the population of Hill's Northwest country.

Hill's name became a symbol of greatness throughout the territory. The settlers blessed him and he grew rich as they prospered. By 1893 he had, one by one, gobbled up the great roads in his part of the country, and both the Great Northern and the Northern Pacific Railway, the largest and most prosperous roads in the Northwest, were under his domination. With the spread of his interests, Hill had combined with J. P. Morgan in the financing of his enterprises, and, in his own territory, met no serious opposition until Edward Harriman cast covetous glances towards that profitable section.

What Harriman lacked in knowledge of the Northwest and its people he made up in an unusual executive ability. Hill was a great builder but Harriman was the more clever financier. So well matched were they in their separate abilities, however, that their great struggle resulted in a drawn battle and a profitable compromise.

II

Edward Henry Harriman was born in Hempstead, Long Island, on February 20, 1848. The son of a clergyman, his interests were from the beginning directed along financial lines, and when family conditions made it necessary for him to go to work, he at once went down to Wall Street for a job. At fourteen he became an office boy for a brokerage firm. The ticker had not yet come into use and the brokers exchanged quotations and bids by means of notations on pads sent from one to the other by boys. These messengers were called "pad-shovers," and young Edward was soon promoted to their ranks. The excitement of the business appealed to the boy and never for a moment did his interest waver. In Wall Street he got his first job and in Wall Street he stayed throughout his life. By 1869, when he was only twenty-one, Harriman was already managing clerk for the Stock Exchange firm of D. C. Hays and Company. The next year he borrowed $3,000 from his uncle, a wealthy New York merchant, bought a seat on the New York Exchange and commenced operating on his own account. His acquaintance in the Street was wide and he soon did a thriving brokerage business. Until 1874 he did a strictly commission business, and

the records of his firm show transactions for leading
operators, Jay Gould and Commodore Vanderbilt
among them. His contact with such men naturally
tempted him to try trading on his own account, and in
1874 he joined an operation to depress the group known
as the "anthracite stocks." The operation was successful and Harriman made a profit of $150,000. Thus
encouraged, he entered alone on an effort to depress
Delaware & Hudson. Unfortunately, the young broker
was not fully conversant with the situation, for without Harriman's knowledge, John Jacob Astor decided
about the same time that this stock was a good buy.
Harriman's short sales naturally had no depressing effect in the face of this powerful accumulation, and he
was soon obliged to cover, taking a loss which wiped
out all his previous profits and cut into his limited capital. This reverse abruptly halted Harriman's market
operations, and for the next two or three years he confined himself once more to the brokerage business ex-
clusively. His profitable commission business gave him
a new capital fund, and in 1878 he purchased a small,
commercial Hudson River boat, as a speculative transaction. Even then, however, he was still timid about
entering any large speculative operation, and his activities along that line involved no great risks. Harriman's marriage in 1879 to Mary Averill, daughter of
the leading banker in Ogdensburg, N. Y., gave him an
acquaintance with the people of that section. His

E. H. HARRIMAN

*An unknown Eastern stock-broker, he fought Hill and
Morgan for control of their Northern Pacific
Railroad, and made them compromise.*

E. H. HARRIMAN

*An unknown Eastern stock-broker, he fought Hill and
Morgan for control of their Northern Pacific
Railroad, and made them compromise.*

wealthy father-in-law had a great deal of confidence in Harriman and offered him financial backing. Two years later he bought a small railroad, 34 miles long, running near Ogdensburg. It had connections with the Pennsylvania and the New York Central, and Harriman bought the line with the intention of reselling it to one of these two larger roads. The company was re-organized as the Sodus Bay & Southern Railroad in 1883 and Harriman soon bought out the other stockholders. The Sodus line was not really necessary to either the Pennsylvania or the Central but each was unwilling to let the other have it. By playing off one against the other Harriman was successful in securing bids from both, and finally sold it to the Pennsylvania at a handsome profit. This venture was so eminently successful that Harriman repeated the process with several other small, strategic roads in the northern part of New York State and each time turned a neat profit.

In Wall Street Harriman was still known as a successful broker, but not one of the men to be considered by the large banking houses in their railroad ventures. He soon came to their notice, however, by a determined struggle against Kuhn, Loeb and Company in their efforts to re-organize the Union Pacific after its difficulties in 1893. Harriman had, a short time before, secured control of the Illinois Central Railroad, one of the smaller roads in the Middle West, and was ambitious to get a hand in the operation of one of the large

Western railroads. In working on the reorganization
plan of the Union Pacific, Jacob H. Schiff, the senior
partner of Kuhn, Loeb and Company, discovered a con-
certed and persistent opposition to his every movement. Schiff thought this opposition came from J. P.
Morgan, who had previously been interested in Union
Pacific, but had given it up as a bad job. Schiff called
on Morgan and suggested that if the latter was interested, Kuhn, Loeb and Company would be glad to
co-operate with his firm in their re-organization plans.
Morgan, in contrast to his usual sound judgment and
foresight, had no faith in the future of the Union Pacific and told Schiff so. He wanted nothing to do with
the plan and volunteered the opinion that it would turn
out to be an unprofitable undertaking. Morgan did,
however, tell Schiff that he would be glad to make inquiries and ascertain the source of the opposition. By
means of the devious intelligence activities of the house
of Morgan it was soon determined that Harriman was
at the bottom of the fight against Kuhn-Loeb's plan.
When Schiff heard this he sent for Harriman. "What is
your purpose in fighting us in this plan?" he asked
Harriman. "I want to get the Union Pacific for myself," was the unexpected reply. Schiff smiled and ended
the conversation. A short time later, however, Schiff
was forced to call Harriman in again. So well organized
was the latter's campaign of opposition, carried on
through the newspapers, the stockholders and even

Congress, that some compromise with Harriman seemed unavoidable if the reorganization plan was to be successfully consummated. Harriman's terms were not modest. He was to be allowed to get a large slice of the road on the same terms as the bankers, and he also demanded that he be made a director and Chairman of the Executive Committee of the new Union Pacific. Schiff was as much a man of honor as a keen banker. Though he saw the necessity of securing Harriman's co-operation, he had already promised the chairmanship to Winslow L. Pierce, who had brought the business to Kuhn-Loeb and had been a leading factor in the preliminary negotiations. Schiff told Harriman as much, assuring him, however, that if he eventually proved to be the strongest man on the directorate he would soon attain an eminent place. On these terms they agreed, and Harriman was permitted to buy $900,000 of the stock on an insider's terms and was elected a member of the Board of Directors. The comparatively uncouth broker was at first coldly received by the other members of the board. Men like Stillman and Pierce were accustomed to colleagues of established financial and social standing. Harriman was an outsider and he was accepted only as a necessary evil. By 1900, Harriman, deeply interested in every detail of the railroad's operation, had proved his value and dominated the policy of the road. He had proved his worth and attained the position he coveted, the chairmanship of the Executive

Committee. During all these years he had been steadily accumulating the stock of the road and by 1900 he was the controlling factor. Together with Kuhn-Loeb he was the Union Pacific. Kuhn-Loeb looked to him as the man at the head of the actual operation of the road, and their co-operation in its management had proved mutually profitable.

James Hill had in the meanwhile been strengthening his hold on the other Northwestern roads. Backed by J. P. Morgan, he had secured control of the Great Northern and the Northern Pacific. He did not look kindly upon the keen competition of the Union Pacific, which Morgan and he had only a few years before refused to take over, and he was seeking some means of preventing its further encroachment on his territory. Both the Hill and the Harriman interests were anxious to secure control of a small road called the Chicago, Burlington and Quincy. Hill and Morgan wanted this road because it would give them a terminus in Chicago for their Northern Pacific. Harriman and Kuhn-Loeb wanted control because the Burlington was a parallel road and a potential competitor of the Union Pacific. They also wanted it in order to keep it out of the hands of the Hill party, and limit their dominance of the territory.

The first organized attempt for control of the Burlington was made by Kuhn-Loeb. Jacob Schiff formed a syndicate composed of George J. Gould, Harriman,

Stillman, then president of the National City Bank, and
his own banking firm. Their objective was to buy 200,-
000 shares of the Burlington in the open market, insuring control, and halting Hill's plan of absorption. The
market operations began in May, 1900, and by June
6 the syndicate had acquired 69,800 shares at an
average price of about $120 a share. At this point they
found that very little stock was coming out at current prices. In the next six weeks they were able to get
only 10,500 shares more, and then the market supply
ran almost entirely dry. Control seemed impossible by
this method of open-market purchase, and in July the
syndicate temporarily suspended operations. They had
by then accumulated 80,300 shares of the Burlington
at a cost of $10,000,000, or an average price of about
$124 a share. In August and September the stock was
inactive. In October, although the syndicate had
stopped buying entirely, the stock suddenly became very
active and rose steadily in price, until in December it
was quoted at $140 a share. Who it was that bought
this stock at the time has never become known. Hill
denied it was he, and pointed out that since he was
during all this time trying to buy the road directly
from its Board of Directors, he would be foolish to
advance the price in the open market and thus increase
the price he would have to pay in private purchase.
The Kuhn-Loeb syndicate gave up entirely the idea of
securing control in the open market and began to

liquidate its holdings. After the mysterious rise it had a large profit on paper. By December 21, it had managed to sell 60,300 shares at an average price of $135 a share, an advance of 21 points over its average purchase price. The remaining 20,000 shares were distributed, 5,000 shares each to the members of the pool, and the syndicate was liquidated. In the meantime, the Morgan and Hill group had been carrying on private negotiations with the Burlington managers, and in March, 1901, were successful in purchasing the road through the Board of Directors, paying the group of majority stockholders $200 a share on behalf of the Northern Pacific Railroad. This step was a direct challenge to the Kuhn-Loeb group, and Schiff and Harriman were not disposed to let their competitors gain the important advantage of control of this key road without a struggle to restore the balance of power.

The retort of the Kuhn-Loeb group to the Hill-Morgan purchase was immediate and dramatic. They set out to get control of the Northern Pacific itself. If they had to, they would buy the mare to get the filly. Schiff first made a formal request to Morgan for a share in the Burlington road. This was, of course, refused, and the battle started.

Of the $80,000,000 in common and $75,000,000 preferred stock outstanding the Morgan interests owned only a total of $35,000,000. With the widely scattered ownership of the stock, this total was then more than sufficient for control. Each form of stock had equal voting power, and Schiff and Harriman started out to buy both the common and the preferred stock of the Northern Pacific on the open market. This operation was started in March, 1901, but so cleverly was it conducted that the Morgan interests did not suspect the move at all for six or seven weeks. Without a single share of stock to start with, Kuhn-Loeb had been able, in two months, to buy $37,000,000 in common and $41,000,000 in preferred stock of the Northern Pacific. This was a clear majority of the total stock, but not a majority of the common alone. Under ordinary circumstances, Kuhn-Loeb control was certain, but an unusual provision in the charter of the road complicated the situation. In the by-laws of the Northern Pacific was a clause calling for the redemption of the preferred, at the option of the company directors, on any January 1st. Schiff was either not aware of this stipulation or else did not consider it a dangerous possibility. However, it turned out to be Morgan's trump card, for the present controlling group, having the majority of the common stock, could redeem the preferred and retain control by virtue of their present holdings.

In May, 1901, Schiff informed J. P. Morgan and Company that his group had control of the Northern Pacific. Morgan himself was abroad. Robert Bacon, in charge of the business of the firm during Morgan's absence, sent a cable after the close of the market on Saturday to Morgan, asking for authority to purchase 150,000 shares of common stock in the open market. Morgan, having just completed the purchase of England's second largest shipping company, was not disposed to let a rival thwart his plans in any direction. His consent was immediately forthcoming, supplemented by instructions to regain control whatever the cost. On Monday morning Bacon gave orders to buy 150,000 shares of Northern Pacific common on the floor at any price. In one day, all his orders were executed, the price of the stock shooting up from 112 to 149¾. The Morgan group then immediately proceeded, through its Board of Directors, to authorize the redemption of the preferred on January 1, 1902, before the next stockholders' meeting. This redemption would leave them in control, as they had the majority of the common stock, which would, after the redemption, be the only form of stock outstanding.

The floor of the Stock Exchange, during this stupendous struggle, was in continual turmoil. The sudden rise of the Northern Pacific attracted large numbers of shorts, who knew little about the meaning of the whole operation, but felt that what goes up must come down. This large short interest suddenly found that no stock was to be had. Morgan and Schiff had taken almost every available share off the market, and in their scramble to purchase, had actually bought a lot of stock that was not in existence. Neither of these

JACOB H. SCHIFF

*He backed Harriman in his market battles, and made
the firm of Kuhn-Loeb a leading banking house
when he successfully disputed Morgan's
imperial powers.*

groups was interested in pressing the shorts, and retired entirely from the market when it was evident
that no more actual stock was available. The price,
meanwhile, kept going up, as frantic sellers tried to
get stock for delivery before the inevitable squeeze
came.

On May 9, 1901, the unintentional corner in Northern Pacific was complete. The stock opened at 170,
an advance of ten points from the close of the previous
day. The short interests desperately tried to cover and
effect delivery before all the market stock was ex-
hausted. The rest of the list on the Stock Exchange
dropped like a plummet, as the shorts threw everything
else overboard, trying to protect themselves while holding out for a better settlement in Northern Pacific. By
twenty minutes after ten Northern Pacific was quoted
at 205. All sales were for cash and the next transactions
were at 225, 230 and 280. Call money went to seventy
per cent. Northern Pacific stock was loaning at a premium of eighty-five per cent, and there was little to be
had even at that figure. A sale for cash came out at
300, then one at 650, 700 and finally one desperate
short bought in at $1,000 a share, cash. The rest of the
market had in the meanwhile dropped 50 to 75 points.
The most conservative securities crashed with the others.
Atchison broke 47 points, Delaware and Hudson 74
points and Union Pacific 57 points. About 2:30 in the
afternoon, Harriman and Hill, as much disturbed at

this debacle as the cornered shorts and unwilling to cause a general disaster by their private battle, announced that they would lend their Northern Pacific to the shorts, pending negotiations for a fair settlement. The market rallied at this news. Call money dropped to forty, in one jump to six, then to three per cent at the close. Total transactions for the day amounted to 3,200,000 shares, shattering all previous sales records. The next morning the Kuhn-Loeb and Morgan groups announced that they would settle with the shorts at $150 a share and the corner was over.

On the main firing line there was a brief armistice. Although Kuhn-Loeb did not have an actual voting majority if the preferred were retired, their majority of both classes of stock gave them a decided legal advantage. For Morgan to retire the preferred, without reference to the rights of the opposing party, would, without doubt, lead to a bitter contest in the courts. At the same time, the Hill-Morgan group could not maintain actual voting control of the Northern Pacific, unless advantage was taken of the redemption clause.

In this situation Morgan decided to let the opposing group in as equals and a compromise was effected. A new company, known as the Northern Securities Company, was organized as a holding company for the stocks of all the roads controlled by the opposing interests. On the board of this new company both groups were equally represented, thus insuring proper protection. With this arrangement the struggle ceased, and the most gigantic open-market battle ever staged in Wall Street for the control of a company was at an end.

CHAPTER XV

CARNEGIE, STEEL AND THE PITTSBURGH
MILLIONAIRES

IN every phase of the economic activity of modern life steel takes a leading part. To-day it shelters us and feeds us. Yet it is only a generation since the country knew anything of steel except as a curiosity. What little of this metal was used in the United States as cutlery was imported from England. In fifty years a group of adventurous pioneers, encouraged by the discovery of the Bessemer refining process, have put this product into almost every item of our industrial civilization. There are now steel cars, steel skyscrapers and steel apartment houses. The farmer uses steel wire to hold his stock and steel agricultural implements to plow his fields. This giant industry was in its infant days nursed, developed and almost monopolized by one group, Andrew Carnegie and his Pittsburgh millionaires.

Carnegie was thirteen years old when he went to work in a cotton-mill as bobbin-boy. His mother took in washing and Andrew's contribution of his princely salary of $1.20 a week was no unimportant part of the

ANDREW CARNEGIE

*The Scotch bobbin-boy who traded closely, dominated
the steel industry, forced Morgan to pay him an
exorbitant price for his plant, and then gave
most of it away saying that "the man who
dies rich, dies disgraced."*

family income. Carnegie had in him even at that early age the seeds of a driving ambition, and a schooling which he sorely missed was supplanted by intensive self-education of a practical nature. By assiduous devotion the boy soon learned something about telegraph operating, and it was not long before he had managed to get a minor job in a telegraph office. By the time he was eighteen Carnegie was a full-fledged operator, and a substantial youth in his community. His calmness and ingenuity in handling communications after a railroad accident attracted the attention of Thomas Scott, then president of the Pennsylvania Railroad, who gave him a job in his office. From the first Scott took a liking to Carnegie and soon made him his private secretary. Carnegie's usefulness to Scott increased as the young Scotchman showed himself competent to handle delicate situations with ability and dispatch. His powers and salary were increased rapidly, and only Scott's fear that Carnegie would be spoiled by a too rapid advancement, prevented promotion to a high executive position. At least that is what Scott said after Carnegie had attained national prominence.

While the able young railroad official was proving his value to the Pennsylvania system Henry Bessemer had finally perfected his process for freeing iron of its impurities. At the same time the discovery was made that steel could be thus produced at a low cost, enormous deposits of iron ore were found in Minnesota. This fortunate sequence of events needed only the proper men to translate it into a mammoth business. Andrew Carnegie, sensing the great possibilities of the infant industry, decided to give up his place in the railroad field and risk a venture into the making of steel.

Carnegie was as canny a diplomat as ever forced his way into the history of American industry. When he decided to leave the Pennsylvania to go into the steel business, in 1875, he called on J. Edgar Thompson who, together with Scott, was now the leading factor in the railroad. Finding it impossible to hold their young protégé, his superiors agreed to help his new venture with their advice. Before soliciting from them more substantial aid in financing his projected enterprise Carnegie announced that his first plant would be called the J. Edgar Thompson Steel Works. Unable to resist either the broad compliment or the remarkable sales ability of young Carnegie, Thompson soon agreed to contribute to the capital of the new firm. Scott also came in with Carnegie, and the financial backing of these men assured the new business a good start. What helped also was the fact that Thompson and Scott gave Carnegie's firm special rebates on its shipments. With this substantial beginning Carnegie was set for a rapid development.

From the very first, Carnegie was little interested in either the manufacturing or the purely financial end of the business. He was essentially a salesman, probably the greatest commercial traveler the United States has ever seen. Business details bored him, but he did not underestimate their importance. While out on one of his whirlwind selling trips, trips which never failed to result in huge orders, Carnegie knew that he must find men who could manage things at the plant. His first "find" was Captain Bill Jones whom he made plant manager with full authority. Jones was a mechanical expert of the first order and process after process was simplified under his able direction. That Jones never became one of the really wealthy men of the country was not the fault of Carnegie, for the latter was from the first a great believer in sharing his profits with his aides. But Jones always preferred to stay in the plant, and consistently refused to discuss with Carnegie the question of participation in the other phases of management or ownership. Jones was interested in the steel works and there he stayed.

To handle the financial end of the business and the routine details, Carnegie got Henry Phipps, a boyhood friend and a genius at figures. Phipps had nothing of Carnegie's sparkle and brilliance, but he could save a dollar as quickly as Carnegie could earn one, and as an economizer and efficiency man he consistently proved his worth. "What we most admired in young Phipps," said a Pittsburgh banker, "is the way in which he could keep a check in the air for three or four days."

Andrew Carnegie once suggested his own epitaph.

"This should be put on my tombstone," he said: "Here lies the man who knew how to get around him men who were cleverer than himself." Not strictly true, for Carnegie, all things considered, was more capable than any of his associates; yet it does indicate Carnegie's reliance on his early partners. Besides Phipps, two other men active in the early development of the Carnegie Company were later taken in, Henry C. Frick and Charles M. Schwab. These men were almost exact opposites. Frick was of a distinctly cold and distant personality, Schwab one of the most warm-hearted and happy-go-lucky men who ever graced a station high in the annals of American industry. The occupations they left to go into the steel business are reflections of their contrasting temperaments—Frick came from a high stool as bookkeeper in his father's distillery, Schwab from the rollicking job of driver of the stage between Loretto and Cresson in Pennsylvania.

When Carnegie asked Henry Frick to join him in 1889 the latter had already become a fairly wealthy man. Frick, when he was only twenty-four, had started purchasing coke mines in Connellsville. He had intense faith in this product and, helped by his father, a man of means, had been successful in buying so many mines that he became known as the "Coke King." Carnegie, at this time, was very much interested in eliminating from his business the purchase of as many as possible of the intermediate products supplied by outside firms, and coke being necessary to the making of steel, he took Frick in as second in command.

Charles Schwab was the youngest man of the group. At the age of eighteen he gave up his stage-driving job and went to work in Carnegie's plant as stake driver at $1 a day. From the very beginning Schwab indicated an unusual ability to ingratiate himself into the good graces of his superiors as well as his fellow employees and this characteristic won him rapid advancement. Strikes were continual occurrences at the works and gradually responsibility for handling the men was turned over to Schwab. After the great Homestead strike it was "Charlie" Schwab, as he was always called both by his associates and his employees, who was given the difficult assignment of patching up the strained relations between the labor force and the management. This he did with a masterly skill. Schwab soon had put into his hands most of the liaison work, both with employees and outside groups, and when he was only thirty-four Carnegie made him president of the corporation.

With Captain Jones beating production records, week after week, Carnegie hustling around and getting tremendous orders and Phipps keeping expenses down, the company found prosperity from the very beginning. With the entrance of Frick and then Schwab as partners its expansion increased and its profits multiplied. While the ordinary business of the company was growing Carnegie missed no opportunity to strengthen his position by collateral expansion. In his efforts to eliminate the middleman Carnegie bought coal mines, limestone, steel ships, railroads and steel mills. So profitable were his policies, and effective his expansion that from 1875 to 1900, the company paid out $133,000,-000 in profits. In 1900 alone $40,000,000 in profits was distributed, of which Carnegie received $25,000,000, Frick $2,600,000 and Schwab $1,300,000.

Carnegie's business methods have, like those of many of America's captains of industry, been severely criticized. Judging from official testimony there is every evidence that his company sold armor plate, produced at a cost of less than $200 a ton, to the United States government at prices ranging from $520 to $700 a ton. What makes this profitable deal seem questionable, to put it mildly, is the fact that, at the same time, Carnegie was selling the Russian government the same quality of armor plate at $249 a ton. A Congressional Committee reported that "the unblushing character of the frauds to which these men have been parties and the disregard for truth and honesty which they have shown . . . renders them unworthy of credence." True it is also that Carnegie took full advantage of special rebates, a practice for which Rockefeller has been most severely condemned. All our story is punctuated with the repetition of such efforts by almost every man who fought his way to the highest peak in

CHARLES M. SCHWAB

*One of the Pittsburgh millionaires whose special
genius was getting along with other people.
Everybody, from Carnegie down to his minor
employees, called him "Charlie."*

industrial activity. Perhaps it was necessity, perhaps the ethics of the period, perhaps a natural perversion of human nature. Whatever the secret methods of the great Carnegie corporation, however, by 1900 it had attained an undisputed dominance in the steel industry in the United States. Carnegie was king of America's most important industry.

At this time, the word gradually spread that Carnegie was ready to abdicate. Cautious inquiries were made by competitors. It was true. To be at the top is often to be lonely. Carnegie had succeeded in business but he began to feel that he might have missed a great deal in life. A few years before he had begun to satisfy his ambition to be a writer. Secretly, he was working, not only on his autobiography, but also on other literary efforts. He had amassed a tremendous fortune, but he didn't know what he could do with it. He had no son to carry on his work, and almost no friends. He had quarreled with Phipps, his one lifelong friend, and there was an estrangement between Frick and himself.

"The man who dies rich, dies disgraced," he announced, and proceeded to give away his money with reckless abandon. Strangely enough, this uneducated man found his greatest interest in libraries and literature. Lonely, discouraged, changed in philosophy, he had retired to the seclusion of his country home to work out a new method of attaining contentment.

It looked like a good time for his rivals to get hold of his business. Two of his competitors actually approached him with an offer. Carnegie asked $157,000,-000. They thought it too high and the deal fell through. The Rockefeller and the Morgan interests were also anxious to crowd Carnegie out. Rockefeller controlled the large Mesaba iron range and with Carnegie's plants could form a powerful trust. Morgan had been forming mergers of competitors in the industry and only Carnegie prevented a virtual monopoly. Rockefeller had long before tried to crush Carnegie by reducing prices; they fought to a standstill, and when Henry Frick approached Rockefeller with the information that Carnegie's plant could now be purchased, he jumped at the chance. Carnegie actually received a million dollars as consideration for an option to Rockefeller and Frick on the purchase of the plants for $100,000,-000. When the time limit drew near Carnegie demanded this in cash, and once again there was no sale. Carnegie refused to return the million, and the antagonism between him and Frick was heightened. Rockefeller was also very angry but said nothing.

Meanwhile J. P. Morgan had been trying to get Carnegie's plants at a bargain price by having the companies under his control go into continuous competition with Carnegie's products, and thus cut into his domination of the field. Carnegie came out from his retirement, put aside his books and stripped for action again. True, he wanted to retire, but no bankers were going to retire him against his will. He was ready to get out, but he wanted to be the one who was to dictate the terms of his honorable withdrawal. Instead of waiting for Morgan to get a foothold in his field he went right out to smash Morgan's companies. One of Carnegie's most important products was billets, which he supplied to the bridge and tube trusts controlled by Morgan, as well as to independents. When these companies announced that they were going to manufacture their own billets Carnegie prepared for battle. Coming down to the center of activity he at once announced that he was immediately entering the bridge and tube business, in which he had never been active. This step might prove a crippling blow to Morgan's present monopoly of that branch of the business. Nor was that all. Carnegie further made public the information that he would at once construct his own railroads from Pittsburgh to the Great Lakes on one side, and from Pittsburgh to New York on the other. The Pennsylvania, a Morgan road, now handled most of this traffic. Whether Carnegie was bluffing is a moot question, but his activities left no time to be lost if he were actually in earnest. Engineering parties were already surveying the route of the newly projected road and Carnegie seemed to be ready for a bitter struggle. Morgan had apparently stirred up the wrong hornets' nest.

Charlie Schwab and John W. Gates were immediately

called in by Morgan for consultation. Schwab, particularly, had been close to Carnegie for years, and knew the man as well as the business. They were both emphatic in advising Morgan not to enter into a struggle with Carnegie in his own field but to buy him out at once at his own price. "Go and ask him what he will sell for," Morgan said. The next day Schwab returned with a letter from Carnegie. The price was set at $492,-000,000, about five times the amount asked from Rockefeller less than five years before. None of this was to be paid in cash, but of the amount a little more than $300,000,000 was to be in bonds and the balance in stock of the new corporation to be organized by the Morgan interests.

Whatever Morgan's earlier mistake was in contesting Carnegie, his action now was decisive. With full knowledge that only a short time before Carnegie had offered to sell out to Rockefeller for only $100,000,000, he accepted at once, and Carnegie became the second richest man in the world. Together with him the many men he had gathered around in the early period of expansion, profited in varying extent. Carnegie's henchmen became the "Pittsburgh millionaires."

Carnegie had asked a tremendous amount for his plants and promptly got it. His pleasure at this coup was somewhat lessened some months later if the story, then current in Wall Street, be true. Carnegie's offer had been accepted so quickly that he later thought he could have got even more money than he actually did. The canny Scotchman was very free with his huge gifts. But he relished, nevertheless, making a deal bring every penny there was in it. He thought many times about this transaction, and when it happened that he and Morgan were on the same liner bound for Europe, he ventured to discuss the matter with Morgan. "Do you know, Mr. Morgan, I have been thinking it over, and I find I made a mistake. I should have asked you another hundred million for those properties." Morgan was frank in his answer. "If you had, I should have paid it." And Carnegie, or so the Wall Street wits like to have it, was so soured in his soul that he could take no more toast and marmalade.

II

When Andrew Carnegie's huge organization came into the hands of J. P. Morgan the last barrier to a great consolidation in the steel industry had been hurdled. Carnegie's group of companies had been the largest single unit in the industry. The only other important plants outside of those controlled by Morgan were in the hands of William H. Moore, an attorney who had made a speciality of reorganizing corporations. He had developed into promotion work and by 1901 controlled four independent steel companies. John W. Gates, popularly known on the Street as "Bet-a-Million" Gates, because of his plunging activities, had previously combined several barbed wire concerns, but had sold out to the Federal Steel Company, under Morgan's control.

With Carnegie out of the way Morgan proceeded to absorb Moore's companies and on Feb. 23, 1901, like a Cæsar recounting his conquests over the barbarians, announced the list of companies which had been gathered into the fold.

Morgan's domination in the steel industry became undisputed. Only the Colorado Fuel and Iron Company and the Tennessee Coal and Iron Company remained without the fold. The Colorado was controlled by the Rockefeller interests, and remained independent, but the Tennessee, weakened in the panic of 1903, was gathered in at a bargain price.

The tremendous profits made by Morgan in the launching of the United States Steel Corporation, have often been the subject of governmental investigation. Only $25,000,000 was risked by Morgan's firm in the enterprise. Under the floor management of Jim Keene, employed by the promoters, the huge enterprise was financed almost entirely by the public, and a clever distribution of the United States Steel securities at its very inception, at once made the symbol X, representing Steel on the ticker, the most important market abbreviation.

The United States Steel Corporation, up to that time,

the greatest achievement in corporate promotion, capped the climax of the combination movement. A consolidation of consolidations, it became the super-trust, the first billion dollar corporation in America.

CHAPTER XVI

J. PIERPONT MORGAN

AMONG all the great princes in the moneyed aristocracy of America, J. Pierpont Morgan stood pre-eminent in his time, as does his son in our generation. In the control of American business before Morgan's time the banker had always been subordinated to the railroad builder, the captain of industry, or the speculator. He was the first banker to wrest control. J. Pierpont Morgan's father, Junius S., was a leading banker and a millionaire. Young Morgan received a thorough academic education, both here and in Germany, and a varied apprenticeship in financial matters.

Morgan is unlike any of the other great characters who enter this story in that he is probably the only one whose origin was not humble. He does not differ from the great majority of the financial leaders of his period in one respect: although twenty-four years old when the Civil War started, the patriotic fever that swept the North did not tempt him to enter the ranks.

At an early age Morgan showed a distinct inclination towards banking activity. In 1861 a certain Arthur M. Eastman purchased from the government 5,000 un-

J. PIERPONT MORGAN

Those he could not crush, he bought.

serviceable rifles at $3.50 each. These rifles were trans-
ferred in title but not paid for nor was delivery effected.
Three months after the purchase the same rifles, although rejected by Washington as dangerous, were sold
to General Fremont for use in the Union Army. When
the order from Fremont was received, calling for the
purchase at $22 each, the rifles were finally paid for by
Morgan at $3.50 each. In a government investigation it
was brought out that J. P. Morgan was backing Eastman in this deal, and as a matter of fact, in subsequent
suits, Morgan actually named himself as principal. This
profitable if shady transaction was J. P. Morgan's first
achievement on his own account.

Eight years later, in 1869, we find the young banker
struggling with Jay Gould and Jim Fisk in a battle for
control of the Albany and Susquehanna Railroad. Morgan's tactics were a match for Jim Fisk, who was per-
sonally supervising the fight, and Fisk finally withdrew from the field. This open battle against such
dangerous opponents first attracted the favorable attention of Wall Street to Morgan.

Young Morgan had in the meantime withdrawn
from his father's old firm, and had, together with another young executive, formed his own banking house.
Dabney, Morgan and Company participated in the Kan-
sas Pacific Railway loan of 1869 as one of the smaller
supporting houses. Morgan's next affiliation was with
the Drexel family, the wealthiest in Philadelphia. With

the formation of the firm Drexel, Morgan and Company, J. Pierpont, although a junior partner, began to take his place among the significant figures in the money world. In 1877, the United States Government floated a loan of $260,000,000 and Morgan, on behalf of his firm and its London connection, J. S. Morgan and Company, was successful in securing entry to the underwriting syndicate. August Belmont, the Rothschilds and J. and W. Seligman were the other participants, the right kind of company for the growing young house. On this flotation Drexel, Morgan and Company was credited with making a clear profit of $5,000,000.

Ten years later, in 1879, Morgan for the first time assumed the leadership among the banking fraternity. William H. Vanderbilt, who had inherited the Commodore's vast properties, had long been troubled by the unusual public animosity against him. The main complaint seemed to be his monopolistic control of the Eastern railroads. Among other companies, he owned almost the entire stock of the New York Central, a road which had become the target for attack both in the press and in the New York Legislature. Other outside circumstances increased Vanderbilt's sensitiveness to these attacks. William H. was not of the same stuff as the sturdy Commodore. If he had once said, "the public be damned" (a statement, by the way, he always denied having made), he did not now feel that way about it. Morgan knew of Vanderbilt's attitude and quietly proceeded to organize a syndicate to purchase Vanderbilt's New York Central stock. The details of this transaction have been previously recorded. Here we might note that the successful consummation of the plan clearly established Morgan's negotiating ability and dominance. What was a further stimulus to Morgan's rise was the fact that this coup gained for Morgan the confidence of Vanderbilt. From that time on Morgan handled almost every transaction involving Vanderbilt's properties, a business which was as profitable as it was important.

Morgan's relations with Vanderbilt had increased the former's interest in the railroads of the country and he set about to inaugurate a new consolidation movement. At first he had confined his activities to smaller roads, buying them up, reorganizing their capital structure, then combining them with competing roads he had quietly purchased and floating public issues of the securities of the combined properties. In 1889 he was ready for a larger deal. On January 2nd of that year a confidential letter was sent to all the great railroad magnates of the country to meet at No. 219 Madison Avenue, Morgan's town residence. The letter was signed by Drexel, Morgan and Company, Brown Brothers and Kidder, Peabody and Company. With these formidable signatures the invitation became a command. Into Morgan's drawing-room came these powers: Jay Gould, followed by his son George; Stickney, of the Northwest roads; Chauncey Depew, representing the Vanderbilts; Sloan of the Lackawanna, and six or seven lesser lights in the railroad world.

A stenographic report of the proceedings gives us a vivid picture of the conference. Morgan presided and at once presented his program. He proposed an organization to be known as the "Interstate Commerce Railway Commission," composed of the leading roads and the bankers represented. Its purpose was, of course, to reduce to a minimum the present competition and to prevent the entry of new competing lines in the field. The bankers would enforce the agreement by the use of their dominant powers. The exact method was briefly outlined by the chairman:

"I am authorized to say, I think, on behalf of the houses represented here, that if an organization can be formed practically upon the basis submitted by the committee, and with an executive committee able to enforce its provisions, upon which the bankers shall be represented, they are prepared to say that they will not negotiate and will do everything in their power to prevent the negotiation of, any securities for the construction of parallel lines, or the extension of lines not approved by the executive committee. I wish that distinctly understood."

The roll was called by railroads and each magnate answered favorably as the name of his road was called.

With the success of this scheme Morgan's leadership in banking circles became undisputed.

In 1890, his father, Junius S. Morgan, died, bequeathing to his son $10,000,000. Soon after, the two Drexel partners of Morgan died and the name of the firm became J. P. Morgan and Company. In 1895, Morgan floated a Government loan for $62,000,000. Purchased by his syndicate at $104 a bond, the entire issue was immediately resold at an average of $119, a transaction which netted the syndicate a quick profit of almost $10,000,000. With this added success in Government financing, all the other Wall Street banking houses began to beseech Morgan for participation in his syndicate. He began to allot shares in his deals to some of his favorite and loyal followers without apprising them of details and sometimes even without consulting their wishes. One house sent a partner around to Morgan to request some details regarding the terms of a loan he was floating in which they were to be permitted to join. "Can't give you any particulars," barked Morgan. "If you want to make some money and have got the gold, subscribe. If not, *au revoir.*"

From 1895 on Morgan's pre-eminence in the banking world became unquestioned as his plans proved increasingly successful. He began to reach out into new fields. From railroads he extended his activities to the large industrial corporations, and his steady acquisition of control in this field was topped by his greatest accomplishment—the formation of the United States Steel Corporation.

From 1901 to the time of his death J. Pierpont Morgan found no opposition to his imperial expansion. Only for a brief period, when Theodore Roosevelt set out on his trust-busting rampage, were his plans ever halted. In this latter period of his active life he began to assume monarchical prerogatives, not only in regard to his own properties but the great corporations controlled by others. If an individual wielding power in some lesser principality on the fringes of his domain did not render due homage to the house of Morgan, he was crushed. If even Morgan could not crush him, he bought him off.

An instance of this policy came to public notice in the case of John W. Gates. Half charlatan and half enthusiast, Gates was in turn a speculator, gambler, builder and destroyer. In 1871, he was a clerk in a hardware store in San Antonio, Texas, working for $25 a month. He had an idea that barbed wire could be used for fencing the Texas steers and tried to sell the idea to the farmers in the cattle country of the Southwestern States. They laughed at his idea and he finally hit on a scheme to convince them. He fenced in a plaza in San Antonio around thirty of the most ferocious Texas cattle he could find. He invited the farmers from miles around to his exhibition. Through this barbed wire fencing not one of the steers could break. The

Photo by Underwood & Underwood

JOHN M. GATES

*"Bet-a-million Gates" was the most colorful plunger
Wall Street has ever seen.*

farmers were impressed and gave Gates's barbed wire a trial.

An excellent salesman, Gates soon had developed a large business and in fifteen years of steady growth had become the head of the American Steel and Wire Company and an important factor in the steel business. When the United States Steel Corporation was formed, he had already sold out to the Federal Steel, and was amusing himself in speculative operations. He saw the unlimited possibilities of the giant merger and tried to get into the Steel Corporation. Morgan would have none of him. Gates was not pleased at this exclusion and prepared a coup designed to irritate Morgan. Knowing that Morgan was anxious to consolidate the Southern Railway system, Gates proceeded quietly to buy up control of the Louisville and Nashville Railroad. It was hard for Gates to do anything quietly but in this case he succeeded. Before the Morgan group could head him off, he had acquired a majority of the stock. Gates didn't know exactly what he would do with this road. He hadn't the slightest conception of railway management. Perhaps Gates expected to be bought off by Morgan. If so, he was right. At three o'clock one morning, George Perkins, a partner in the Morgan firm, banged at Gates' room in the Waldorf-Astoria. Morgan had just learned that Gates had control of the Louisville and Nashville.

They wanted no such mischief-maker in the way,

[297]

for the Morgan group was just in the midst of an attempt to consolidate the important Southwestern roads. Gates was a dangerous man and they wanted him out at any price, at least for a time. They would watch him more closely after that. Gates was half asleep when Perkins unceremoniously walked in and, in response to a demand for his price, Gates told Perkins that he would sell out if Morgan would give him a $10,000,000 profit on his operation. Gates was just talking in order to get his bearings, and he could scarcely believe it when he heard Perkins say: "Agreed, the road is ours." The great success of Gates in this operation tempted him to try a similar one soon after. But Morgan was now out to get him; when Gates came into the market this time, Morgan's forces were watching, and without much ceremony they crowded the colorful plunger to the wall. Under Morgan's attacks the prestige of the greatest plunger Wall Street has ever known began to recede. The active speculative life of the man who was reputed to have bet $1,000,000 on the progress of a fly on a window pane was coming to an end.

In the panic of 1907 the house of Morgan came to the relief of the money market and supported prices. Its interests had become so large and so manifold that any shock to the financial structure of the country was a direct disturbance of its property values. With the birth of the twentieth century its control had extended to the insurance companies and commercial

Photo by Ewing Galloway

THE PRESENT OFFICES OF J. P. MORGAN AND
COMPANY ON WALL STREET

banks. The greatest banking house in the world began to absorb other moneyed institutions. This pyramid of money control makes the present Morgan generation the most powerful single financial group in the world. Its power is none the less imperial because it is not too openly flaunted. Like the great powers of the Middle Ages it has gathered around it many loyal potentates of lesser principalities whose fealty and support enhance and strengthen the sovereign power of the great house of Morgan.

CHAPTER XVII

HENRY FORD, WILLIAM DURANT, THE FISHER
BROTHERS AND THE AUTOMOBILE

THE attention of Wall Street in the early 1900's shifted from one giant merger to another. Following upon the great success of the Standard Oil Company, the steel, the tobacco, the agricultural implement and the metal and mining interests entered into massive consolidations. Hardly a day passed without the announcement of a new flotation, and the Street accepted each one as a promise of greater things. The large banking houses of the East were replacing individuals as the prime movers in these enterprises, and no captain of industry, however original his scheme, integrated his accomplishments or substantiated his personal credit, but was forced to present himself at the inner sanctum of the house of Morgan or Kuhn-Loeb to assure completion of his plans. Amidst this excitement, a group of hopeful men, one Henry Ford among them, started a small company called the Detroit Automobile Company. No Eastern banker was approached, so useless did such a step appear for this risky venture in a virgin field. The group of Detroit merchants

Photo by Brown Brothers

HENRY FORD

He offered to sell out for $8,000,000 in 1908.

which launched the company was determined to get a model ready in time for the first New York Automobile Show in January, 1901. Henry Ford was the engineer and he proceeded to his original task with thoroughness but not sufficient haste to suit his financial backers. After an original appropriation for his expenses of $10,000 had been run up to $86,000 Ford was asked to resign. Strangely enough the company proceeded to get much better results under other engineering management, and Alanson Brush, who succeeded Ford, managed to get his model ready in time for the show, and at a minimum expense. Under the leadership of Henry M. Leland, the name of the company was soon changed to the Cadillac Motor Car Company, and long before Henry Ford could get results, their model was the sensation of the New York show.

In the meanwhile Ford wasted no time. On Nov. 23, 1901, the Henry Ford Automobile Company was formed with a capital of $38,000. This company did not last long, for Ford, even as in later and more prosperous days, could not get along with his stockholders. He wanted a low-priced car; they wanted a car of high price. For more than a year Ford hunted capital to start a new company, and on June 15, 1903, the Ford Motor Company was organized, with Ford holding 255 shares of a total issue of 1,000. The book capitalization was $150,000, but actually only $28,000 was put up in cash by the original group. Among the twelve Ford pioneers were the Dodge brothers, later builders in their own right, James Couzens and A. Y. Malcomson. Couzens scraped together $1,000 and gave the company his note for $1,500. Twenty years later his investment was worth more than $25,000,000.

Just as the story of Rockefeller has become the story of oil, so has the story of Henry Ford become the romance of the automobile business. In Couzens and Malcomson Ford at last found men who were sympathetic with his plans and able to relieve him of all responsibilities outside of production. From the first the new company prospered. Ford's early experiences with his former backers had so turned him against men purely financial in their interests that never since has he welcomed banking participation in his company. For *his* company it soon became. One by one, as his resources increased, he bought out the other original stockholders. By 1908 only Couzens was standing by in active participation. Business had prospered steadily, but the years of steady and arduous labor were telling on Ford's constitution. He was harassed also by many patent suits, which diverted his energy and disturbed his mind. The financial genius of the automobile business was William C. Durant, as daring and ingenious a promoter as Wall Street has ever seen. Durant had been one of the first to grasp the tremendous financial possibilities of the automobile business, and had been the

WILLIAM DURANT

*The great bull of our time. He often bites off more than
he can chew. But he always comes back.*

first man to introduce consolidation in the industry. He heard of Ford's condition and distress and though he possessed little capital made a determined attempt to buy out Ford. "How much will you pay?" asked Ford. Durant offered $8,000,000. "All right," said Ford, "but cash on the table." Durant went back to the Board of Directors of his newly organized General Motors. The board was ready to back him, but the company's bankers were skeptical. "The Ford business isn't worth that much money," they told him. And Durant just missed, as he did so many times in his life, the realization of a dream.

The weak roots of the giant industry soon strengthened and grew. By 1908 men of the caliber of Olds, Winton, Packard, Chalmers and Chapin had become interested. Walter P. Chrysler, then shop superintendent of the Chicago Great Western Railroad, put his entire savings of $700 into an automobile so he could study its parts.

The rest of the story of the Ford Motor Company is so unrelieving in its steady tale of prosperity that it almost loses interest, except for its magnitude. Ford alone, of all the early *entrepreneurs* in the field, studiously avoided bankers, to his great profit. In his book, *My Life and My Work*, he has this to say on the subject:

"I determined, absolutely, that never would I join a company in which finance came before the work or in which bankers or financiers had a part. . . . The new equipment and the whole progress of the company have always been financed out of earnings."

William C. Durant, in 1929 still alive and increasingly active, both in the automobile business and even more so in general financial operations, has always been in league with bankers, and often in difficulties as a result. He had gone through a trying apprenticeship. He had been an errand boy for a grocery, common laborer in a mill, clerk in a cigar store and salesman for a waterworks. His is a restless mind and an optimistic nature not hindered by remorseless facts. While working as a salesman he came to the abstract conclusion one day that there was money in building road carts. Coming upon a small plant he offered the owner $2,000 for it. The offer was accepted immediately, and Durant was in the vehicle business. That is, if he could raise the $2,000, a feat extremely difficult for a youth without a nickel to his name. He went to Flint where he was known, and finally cajoled a friend of his into giving up $1,000. Not a penny more could he raise. But Durant was always a good talker. He proceeded to take over the business. "You'll get the rest of the money in a few months," he told the former proprietor. Durant's partner was J. D. Dort, and together they made a perfect combination. Dort took over the manufacturing end and Durant handled the sales and financing. Restless, brilliant, daring and resourceful, Durant was to see the carriage business extend to fourteen plants. He then went out for bigger game. By 1903, he was manager at the Buick plant and a large stockholder of the company. By 1908, he had consolidated the Cadillac, Oakland and Oldsmobile companies into the General Motors Company. He paid more than the companies were worth, and he knew it, but he always itched for a new deal, a bigger field. He himself said of the Oldsmobile Company purchase: "It's a hell of a price to pay for a lot of road signs." But Durant was always overextending himself. He was always buying things he couldn't pay for, always confident that the money would come forth when needed. When he was dealing with the carriage builder, he managed. But not always when he got in with the Morgans and the other big banking groups. By 1910, Durant had gathered twenty-four other companies of various values and all descriptions into the fold. This was General Motors. Among them were many worthless companies, for which Durant paid millions. The bankers stepped in, and power though he had been, Durant was forced out of the company for five years. Then he marshaled new forces, and regained control of General Motors only to lose it again. Durant, out of General Motors, was not yet beaten. In New York they soon heard that he had purchased a small automobile plant, manufacturing an almost unknown make of car called the Chevrolet. He bought also the Republic Motor Company in Tarrytown, and reorganized it to make Chevrolets there. In 1914 and 1915 he produced 16,000 cars, and was ready to stage a new fight to regain control. He got his figures together, got out his best selling talk, and went to see Pierre S. du Pont, up to that time not at all interested in the automobile business. His conversations were conducted mainly with a young man named John J. Raskob, secretary to Mr. du Pont. Raskob was impressed and urged a connection with Durant. This suggestion was accepted, and early in 1915, Durant, du Pont and Louis G. Kaufman, president of the Chatham and Phenix National Bank, began buying into General Motors. On Jan. 2, 1915, General Motors was selling at 82. It went to 100, to 125, to 250. Shorts were routed, they covered and withdrew, and still it went up. And there were few who knew where the buying came from. The Chevrolet Company was then capitalized at $100,-000. In September, 1915, announcement was made of an increase in capitalization to $20,000,000. Seven million dollars in stock was immediately floated, and the magic of Durant's name resulted in an oversubscription of ten times the issue. The balance of unissued Chevrolet stock Durant offered to General Motors stockholders in exchange for their present holdings at a ratio of five to one. By now, the powers which had replaced Durant in control of General Motors realized his objective, but so fired was the imagination of the public by Durant's achievements, that it was useless to try to stop the pop-

WALL STREET IN 1908

ular stampede into the Durant camp. The General
Motors management enlisted the aid of some of the
most powerful banking groups in New York to fight
Durant. Charles H. Sabin, Albert Strauss, Albert H.
Wiggin, Emory Clark, men of the greatest power in
the banking fraternity, signed circular letters to the
stockholders urging them to continue the present management. Meanwhile Durant increased the Chevrolet
Company stock to $80,000,000 in common. By May,
1916, he notified the directors of General Motors that
he had control. After five years of struggle, William C.
Durant, the greatest bull since Commodore Cornelius
Vanderbilt, returned to the president's chair that he
had relinquished reluctantly five years before. Again
Durant started out for bigger things, biting off more
than he could chew, trying to chew more than he could
swallow. Company after company was purchased at
any price. For a few years he reigned. But his structure, magnificent as it was in conception, bold as it
was in formation, was not solid in foundation. The
lean years of 1920 and 1921 found General Motors
reeling. The following of a man like Durant is enthusiastic but not faithful or dependable. Rumors of
difficulties began to spread and General Motors stock
went whirling down. The market broke to $40 a share.
When it reached 30 Durant organized a pool to support the stock. Like his great predecessor, the Commodore, he sat at his desk at this trying time, and hurled

defiant orders to "Buy! buy! buy!" But down went the stock to 20. Still he bought. Wildly, foolishly, stubbornly, he bought every share offered. He held off for a day, and down it went again to 18, to 17, to 15, to 14, to 12. His telephones were now silent. Brokers called for instructions in vain. No answer. Durant had stopped buying. He was broke.

On Dec. 1, 1920, he walked into the offices of the General Motors Company, said "good-bye" and tendered his resignation, leaving the shattered hulk to the piloting of Pierre du Pont, John J. Raskob, whose interest in the company he had originally enlisted, and Alfred P. Sloan jr., whom he had discovered and later brought forward to a leading position. Durant at sixty, millions in debt, discredited, was not through even now. Incorrigible optimist, resourceless fighter that he was, there was no defeat for him save death. A new stock soon came into the market—Durant Motors. Canvassers travelled from door to door selling one and two shares—and not two years passed before "Billy" Durant was back in public esteem. To-day, he is the king of the stock market, the god of the small trader and the bulwark of the bulls. Still optimistic, still plunging, he is reported as having lost $20,000,000 in the temporary crash early in 1929. True or not, there is no question that so long as he lives Durant will skate on thin ice. For no matter how much he has, it is the nature of the man to wander into new fields, seeking

THE SIX FISHER BROTHERS

A major force in the stock market today. Members of the "Big Ten."

greater obstacles to hurdle, larger trees to fell, new forests to conquer and subdue.

Rising above the many capable, if lesser figures in the business are Henry Ford in the manufacturing end, William Durant in the financial manoeuvres and Fisher Brothers in the sound commercial development. This interesting group of six Fisher brothers, working together from the very first in amicable and efficient cooperation, built up an industry allied with and essential to the automobile.

It has frequently been said that had there been no Fisher Body, there could have been no General Motors. The great corporation which bears their name was started in Norwalk, Ohio, as a carriage-making shop by the father of the present dynasty of six Fisher brothers. In this little shop the eldest two brothers served their apprenticeship. Fred J. Fisher, the oldest brother, was the first of the family to realize the possibilities of the growing automobile business. Before he was thirty he was manager of the Wilson Body Company in Detroit. By 1908, he felt that his experience warranted a venture on his own account, and with his brother Charles T. organized the Fisher Body Corporation with a capitalization of $50,000. One by one, the other brothers were taken into the business. Each was assigned a different department, and the family comprised a complete management unit. Among the brothers, the necessary experience was developed to handle entirely the manufacturing, distribution and financial ends of the business. No outsider was in any important executive position, and so successful had this family organization been that by 1918 their firm was in almost complete control of the body-building business. In that year they made a very favorable arrangement with General Motors for the supply of all their bodies, and by 1923 the arrangement developed into a complete consolidation. To-day the resources of the Fisher brothers are estimated to be more than $500,000,000, and the empire of Fisher interests is expanding rapidly into other industries.

The Fisher Body Company is in itself a great achievement. More important is their recent control purchase of many of the largest companies in the United States. Buying to hold, they have quietly bought into such basic and important properties as Baldwin Locomotive, Westinghouse Electric, Texas Oil and New York Central. To-day the Fisher brothers are perhaps the most prominent group in the stock market. They are not manipulators. Buying to hold, they sometimes control. But always they are extending their interests and consolidating their investments. It is not a rash prediction to venture that not many years will pass before their family fortune will equal even the giant accumulations of the Rockefellers, so steady is their advance and so well organized their measured growth. Not until they see fit to make public announcement does any one know where their new interests lie. Not many months pass, however, without the placing of a Fisher representative on the directorate of another substantial company. Their holdings are varied in nature, but always in sound, growing enterprises. Without fanfare they are developing an impressive accumulation of holdings, ever extending their power and strengthening their dominant position in American industry.

CHAPTER XVIII

THE WAR AND WALL STREET

THE clouds that hovered over Europe's political horizon in the summer of 1914 were watched by no group more closely than the financial interests. As ever, investors and traders throughout the world wavered with every change in atmosphere. With the last days of July, as the probability of conflict became more pronounced, liquidation of holdings became marked. Support was lacking, and by the 27th of the month, before any actual overt act of war, selling had become so urgent that Vienna, Budapest, and Brussels closed their bourses. The liquidation by frightened investors became cumulative as the crisis approached, and before the end of the month every large exchange in Europe was closed. All this time the New York Stock Exchange continued daily trading and bore the brunt of the financial crisis. Foreign holders were encouraged by their governments to convert their securities into gold, in anticipation of their needs at home. The New York market broke day by day, and on July 31st, 1914, when the closing of the London Exchange became public, prices dropped an average of twenty points. On the same day, after the close of the market, an emergency conference was called at the offices of J. P. Morgan and Company. The leading bankers and the directing officials of the Stock Exchange gathered there. After a protracted discussion, it was decided to keep the Exchange open. Before the members of the group had dispersed, however, it was announced that a committee representing several large houses with foreign connections wished to place some facts before the officials. They showed batches of newly arrived selling orders from abroad. The orders represented a tremendous amount of securities. They were orders at the market, and those which placed a limit made it from fifteen to twenty points below the close. With these additional facts, the officials and bankers decided to reconsider the matter and meet again the next morning for a vote on means of averting the inevitable crash. At four minutes before ten, the tickers announced that the New York Stock Exchange would suspend trading for an indefinite period. That day the gong did not ring at the opening for the first time since 1873, when Jay Cooke's crash disabled the machinery.

Brokers who were members of the Exchange were forbidden to trade or execute commissions until further notice, and as every out of town exchange followed suit, the market for securities was almost entirely suspended. For a few days, the financial community, stunned by the sudden decision, ceased activities. But gradually brokers not under the supervision of Exchange officials began to exchange quotations, and the so-called "gutter market" was started on New Street. Quotations were far below the closing prices on the Big Board, and they continued to decline as country after country joined the conflict.

While the exchanges of the country had ceased to function, the plans for inaugurating a central control of the banking system were being intensively developed. On November 16, 1914, the Federal Reserve Bank started active operation.

During all this time frequent meetings were held to determine whether it was safe to reopen the Exchange. Finally, on Saturday, December 12, 1914, the officials announced the resumption of trading under a temporary protective plan. Prices for all the active stocks were set by Exchange officials just below the closing on July 31st and no trades were to be permitted under that figure. Thus, the quotation for United States Steel was fixed at $48 a share. This plan was not satisfactory, as bids were not available at the minimum prices set, and the market entered a period of dullness. The price limit of steel was reduced to $43, then to $40, and finally to $38. Only at this figure and similar limits in other stocks was actual trading in any volume resumed.

Until April, 1915, the market continued in a state of dullness and depression. The foreign Governments began about that time to contract for purchases of large amounts of war supplies in the United States, and the stimulus of this business soon overcame the bearish conditions. Operations for the rise began in earnest, and stock after stock was whirled up on war profits rumors. The swift ascent of the "war-babies" startled the market into a fresh activity.

From then until the entrance of the United States into the war, the position of the market was based almost solely upon war developments. In contrast to the depression that attended the first rumors of war, every sign of peace was now the signal for a burst of selling, for the prosperity of many American industries was believed dependent upon the continuation of foreign war orders. Many coups were engineered on the basis of war news. Of these, only one need here be considered as an example of such manipulation, both because of its scope, and because a central figure was Bernard M. Baruch, one of the keenest in-and-out traders who ever operated on the Street.

On the evening of December 20, 1916, Secretary of State Lansing made public a peace note which President Wilson had just sent to the belligerents. For a few days before that time, there had been intensive short selling of securities by important trading interests. The news of this short selling became public and resulted in a Congressional investigation to determine whether there had been a leak. Bernard Baruch's testimony gives us a good picture, both of the Street's interpretation of the news from Europe and the actual details of a large operator's transactions. It had been rumored that Mr.

Baruch had made a profit of $6,000,000 in the ten days between December 10th and the 20th, but the testimony fixed $476,186 as the exact amount on the turn. Mr. Baruch's testimony is given in full:

"On December 11, I was long on various stocks which appear on brokers' accounts only, and also on stocks which I sold outright. In the period from December 11 to December 15 I sold these securities, amounting, in long stocks, to about 30,000 shares, besides about 25,000 or 26,000 shares short. The zenith of this selling was apparently reached on December 14, when I was short 25,000 shares of Steel. On the 15th I had bought in 14,000 shares."

"Take Steel all through," said Mr. Whipple. "What were your transactions?"

"On December 11th," said the witness, "I was long about 5,000 shares at the close. Most of them were bought that afternoon. On the 12th I sold this stock, probably late in the afternoon, I think, through H. Content and Company. I had none at the close. I bought it at 123 and a fraction and sold at 119 and a fraction. I remember that well enough."

"I'm sorry, Mr. Baruch," said Mr. Whipple. "The world believes you never had a loss. Now, what other stocks—"

"It was the same with Rubber," said Mr. Baruch; "with Ray Copper, Chile Copper, Cuba Cane Sugar preferred; some of that I already had. I got rid of them as soon as I could, though apparently it took two or three days to get rid of all of them."

Q.—Did you go short on any stocks on this day? A.—Canadian Pacific—I was short on that all the time.

Q.—What did you do in Steel on Dec. 13? A.—I sold 23,400 shares, starting early in the day.

Q.—Why? A.—I think the reason should be apparent to every one, but I'll tell you.

"I'd have started earlier," the witness said, "but I was out all day. When I read Chancellor von Bethmann-Hollweg's speech in the Reichstag, which, after the greatest war in civilization, was a declaration of peace, I realized what this meant to the world, and particularly to the world of business and finance. I thought that the people's minds, which heretofore had been bent on war, were now turned to peace. My mind worked to the conclusion that a man of intelligence would ack quickly and sell securities."

"Was there any other reason for selling short?" asked Mr. Whipple.

"I knew that the technical condition of the market was bad, but the real thing was the body-blow of this speech, which still hangs like a pall on the whole situation."

"Why should peace affect the market unfavorably?"

"My personal opinion, which is perhaps the reflection of many others, is that our country has had, I might say, a false prosperity. We had got an enormous business whose profit was out of all ordinary proportions. Peace would bring with it reaction and the opening of an era of other activities. From the humane standpoint I take a different view; but peace would raise trouble with the stock market."

"Was the rise of money rates regarded as a danger signal?"

"I should think it would be. There was no other factor besides the technical condition of the market and the Chancellor's speech which affected my course on those days. The 23,400 shares which I sold on the 13th went at about 118½. On Monday I had bought them at 123.

"On Dec. 14 I went short more than 1,600 shares of Steel. On the 15th the market broke and I bought nearly 14,000 shares around 110. On the 18th, Monday

(Saturday's dealings, since no shares are delivered on Saturday, are included with Monday's on the account sheet), I sold again about 4,000 shares. So I was short about 15,000 shares of Steel at the close."

"Can you remember why you did this?" asked Mr. Whipple.

"Because the market commenced to go up."

"Why should you sell when the market was going up?"

"Because I wanted to hear the next great thing, Lloyd George's speech, and I thought he would say about what he did say. I thought he would leave a door open for peace, and that this would have almost as great an effect as the other. You can't get away from the Bethmann-Hollweg note. Everybody would think about peace after that."

"What about the 19th?" asked Mr. Whipple.

"I sold 28,400 shares."

"Why?"

"I remember very distinctly," said Mr. Baruch. "The first part of the day I read some private dispatches from abroad on the Dow-Jones ticker—I think two banking houses were named. The first part might be considered as meaning that Lloyd George wouldn't listen to peace. As the market rose I sold at first. I was standing at the ticker, and as soon as I saw that he had left a door open for peace I sold as fast and as hard as I could. I was astonished to find that people didn't realize the meaning of his speech, and looked on it as a mere news item. The same thing happened in the wheat market, I understand, as in the Stock Exchange."

"In your operations on that day," said Mr. Whipple, "were you affected in the slightest degree by any news from Washington as to the attitude of the Administration?"

"Absolutely not at all. I didn't receive any such news."

Q.—How about the 20th of December? A.—I bought

17,900 shares, making my short account 26,500. I bought on the scale down, acting on my own judgment. It was a very unfortunate judgment, for the next day the market broke five or ten points.

Q.—If you had known that something would happen the next day which would break the market, what would you have done? A.—I would have sold, all day long.

Q.—Was this a large transaction for you? A.—I have done bigger ones, where I was operating in only one stock.

Q.—Do you regard it as a major operation? A.—A fair-sized one. Do I have to tell you what I've done in other transactions? I'll tell you if you ask.

But nobody asked him. Mr. Whipple went on to the transactions of Dec 21.

"I took everything in," said the witness. "I bought it all in before noon, at an average of 106 for Steel. It seems that I never get in at the bottom, or at the top."

"Had you closed all your transactions by the time Mr. Lansing made his announcement?"

"I think I was long in the market—not in Steel —by that time."

"When I want to buy," Mr. Baruch continued, "I buy what I most believe in from the intrinsic standpoint. I was holding 14,000 more shares that night than the night before."

"How about your dealings on the 22d?"

"I disposed of my holdings again."

"Why?"

"Because, Mr. Whipple," said Mr. Baruch vigorously, "we're going to have peace. Germany wants it, and every man in the world wants it if he can get it on honorable terms. They may not get it to-morrow or the next day, but if the people are thinking about a thing and want it they'll probably get it. I may be absolutely wrong, but this is my opinion."

The note which Wilson sent to the warring powers, effective as it was in giving some large operators an opportunity for a turn, did not succeed in paving the way for a reconciliation, and securities soon resumed their upward course. With the entrance of the United States into the war in April, 1917, there was a simultaneous initiation into security purchasing by a great horde of persons. The Liberty Bond campaigns had educated this public, and the market soon began to feel the force of this influx. The manager of a large brokerage house described the resulting book as the pikers' market. "Every piker in Christendom," he said, "has broken into Wall Street with his shoe-string." This increased public participation has every year multiplied the trading transactions on the floor, until in 1929 the first 8,000,000 share day became a fact. The knowledge of actual conditions among this group is negligible, and trades are made on the basis of what "they" are saying or doing. This inclusive term, impressive if indefinite, is taken to mean the large operators of the day, the group sometimes referred to as the "Big Ten." Whether it is William Durant, or Jesse Livermore, or Arthur Cutten, or the Fisher Brothers, or John J. Raskob, or one of the more temporary leaders is unimportant to the man on the outside. Most of them learn sooner or later that old Daniel Drew was right when he said, "To speculate in Wall Street when you are not an insider is like buying cows by candlelight."

CHAPTER XIX

THE BLOODLESS REVOLUTION

WHERE once wandered a few amiable families of stray pigs, there now are herded together the men who pull the strings that move the world. Further and further have the imperial rulers of Wall Street extended the boundaries of their territory and more and more do all the lesser financial principalities look to New York for guidance and instruction. The force that is in the hands of a few strong men is powerful enough to dwarf and engulf even the power of the greatest of hereditary monarchs. Those who have felt its pressure know its force. That the rule of Wall Street is wise and beneficent is all that prevents its mammoth power from being more widely appreciated and feared.

Since 1890, the beginning of the period of great amalgamations, the secret levers of all the great industries in the United States have been concentrated in the money center. Since 1914, the great power station has added the levers of all the other and lesser financial capitals of the world, and its dominance to-day is as centralized as it is undisputed.

[331]

THE STORY OF WALL STREET

In the years since 1920, a new influence has come into the industrial and financial world. Initiated by Liberty Bonds, made prosperous by the war, and conscious of a new means of getting rich without working, the new army of the middle class has borne down upon Wall Street. Fleeced time and time again by the experienced operators of the Street, its hordes have each time returned in larger force, with capital easily renewed in a prosperous industrial country, and have once again laid siege to the battlements. The United States had developed a prosperous middle class, large in numbers, but as yet unconscious of its latent power. Contrary to the prediction of Karl Marx that the middle class would be crushed and extinguished in the furious struggle between the upper and lower classes, this group has, in the United States, gained in numbers, in power, and in confidence. Surplus funds, small in individual cases but tremendous in the aggregate, have been placed by these persons in the stocks of American corporations. By 1922, it has been estimated by H. T. Warshow, in the first statistical investigation made of this tendency, more than 15,000,000 persons in the United States were owners of stocks. Strangely enough this development has strengthened rather than weakened the hold of the large financial interests on American industry. For so widely have the stocks of national corporations become distributed, that the management and the ownership of these huge businesses are no longer

JOHN J. RASKOB

*He induced DuPont to buy into General Motors, and thus
started his own rise to eminence in the financial world.*

synonymous. It has now become possible for financiers to control and manage large industries with very little stock ownership, since the small stockholders—the real owners of the business—are scattered and unorganized. The hold of the money powers upon American industry has become still more certain and centralized, though now there looms the ever-present possibility of organized opposition from the smaller investing class.

The last few years have seen a rapid development of a form of financial organization comparatively new to America. The investment trust idea has long been used in England. Here its institution has been rapid and popular. Giving even the very small investor the opportunity of diversifying his holdings and distributing his risk, it has made common stocks seem less risky to the careful person. In its effect the investment trusts have not shifted the balance of the present money powers, however, since it is they who have organized and are controlling the largest of these aggregations. This form of organization lends possibilities to a new type of financial leader. John J. Raskob recently announced plans for the formation of a huge investment trust whose stock would be issued in very small units and whose scope would be designed to attract millions of stockholders in this one venture. Successfully launched under the personal leadership of one man, or even a group of men, it would result in the formation of a concentrated money force that would be second in power only to the Government. And were it to attain the confidence of a large proportion of the middle-class investors, its impress might be made even on our national Government. Political, financial, and social measures might be weighed by this group in the light of their specific interests and the opinions of their leaders. Such a group, carefully organized and skillfully guided, would be the only power capable of dwarfing the present moneyed interests. They could even name Presidents, declare war, and enact legislation as their interests decreed. And carried to its ultimate logical effect, this tendency might result in a levelling influence arising from the apparently contradictory process of a vast accumulation of capital.

We are even now in one of the most important periods of change in the country's financial history. In no previous period, as compared with the last ten years, have there been such extensions of interest by newer groups. Almost every man above the class of laborer is practically interested in the gyrations of the market. With this new group the chances of operators to turn a certain profit from market manipulations are lessening. For so many new and uncontrollable factors enter into the rise and fall of stocks that only men of the greatest wealth can be certain of effecting their ends by market operations. A manipulation to-day to be successful must be managed in hundreds of thousands of shares, to eliminate the chance of conflict with the general public purchasing or selling against the operators' plan. Only two or three groups, like the Morgan and Rockefeller combinations, can now direct the course of the market without reference to this outside force. The market has become a national plaything. Much of the public speculation is frivolous and foolhardy. But in spite of this there is enough of a sound basis to this movement to prove the fact that the middle class is actually accumulating and holding many of the stocks it buys. And this movement, growing in force and widening in scope, may yet be the means of the conquering of the United States by the middle class. We may even now be in the midst of this bloodless revolution.

CHAPTER XX

THE DEVELOPMENT OF THE EXCHANGE

IT is now a hundred and forty-two years since that memorable day in May, 1792, when the twenty-four original members of the New York Stock Exchange drew up their first agreement. That pioneer group has gradually been developed into a powerful organization, wielding a tremendous influence in our economic civilization. In its fundamentals, the New York Stock Exchange to-day follows the same guiding principles laid down by its founders. Organized as a voluntary organization or a club, it retains its exclusive nature, successfully resisting alike the efforts of outsiders to dictate its policy or of governmental agencies to supervise its activities. In the last hundred years, powerful corporations, both industrial and banking, have been forced to yield to the supervision of outside forces, social and governmental. The Exchange alone, of all the varied institutions growing out of a highly developed money organization, has been permitted to operate a business involving billions of dollars of the public's money, without the slightest intrusion of any power outside of its nominated officials. Nor is the

situation accidental. The resistance of the Exchange
to outside pressure has been successful only because its
internal operation is recognized to be as careful, and the
supervision of its own members as rigid as any legal
control could make it. The valuable privileges which
its members possess have been jealously guarded from
abuse, and the efficiency of its service has always kept
pace with the public necessity.

The first group which met under the buttonwood
tree remained in the open air for twenty-five years. Not
until 1817, when the first constitution of the body of
brokers was drawn up, was inside space secured. Chairs
were then provided for the members, for in 1817, a
"seat" on the Exchange was actually a chair, and not
only a term designating privileges. The peregrinations
of the restless group until 1842 have previously been
described. In that year, a large hall was finally obtained
in the Merchants' Exchange Building, situated on the
present site of the National City Bank. Here the New
York Stock and Exchange Board remained until 1854.
Seats had not as yet attained exchangeable value. Social
station and general desirability were the main require-
ments for admission at that time. And apparently the
members still remembered the fact that their organization then, as it still is to-day, was founded as a social
club.

It was only after the Civil War that a continuous
market in securities was put into effect. Up to that time,

stocks and bonds were "called" at intervals during the
day, and trading in any particular stock was limited to
the period of the "call." The membership of the Board
had been increased only slowly, but with the gradual
increase in members, brought about even against the
organized resistance of the vested constituency, the
Board had, by 1867, attained a membership of 533. In
that year, for the first time, the stock ticker was introduced, and the Exchange entered upon its policy of
giving widespread publicity to its activities.

The speculative mania which swept the country after
the Civil War resulted in a rapid increase in the volume
of business. Thirty-one-share days had passed forever.
The keen young men who clamored for admission to
the exclusive company of Exchange brokers were not
satisfied to let this profitable business be monopolized,
and a group who were unsuccessful in obtaining admission to the Old Board, as it was soon called, formed
an independent organization in 1864. This they called
the Open Board of Brokers. Still another group formed
an exchange they called the Government Bond Department, devoted solely to dealing in United States Government securities. These competitive organizations for
a time divided the growing business with the Old Board,
and in 1869, the senior organization, influenced by its
younger members, amalgamated with the two outside
groups. At this time, the Stock and Exchange Board
had 533 members, the Open Board 354, and the Gov-

ernment Bond Department 173. All these members were taken in on equal terms, and the combined strength amounted to 1,060. At this figure the membership remained until 1881, when 40 "seats" were sold to defray the expense of getting additional quarters. At the figure of 1,100, membership of the Exchange remained until 1928, when the large increase in sales volume due to a record public participation, led the Board of Governors to increase the membership to 1,375.

The unusually large prices paid in our times for "seats" on the Exchange is a comparatively recent development. In the '60's, it was usual to value a membership only at the cost of initiation, then $1,000. By 1871, however, we find record of a sale at $2,750. In the boom year of 1882 the price reached $32,500, but the panic of 1884 brought the quotation down again to $20,000. The price from that time on to 1893 fluctuated, a high record of $34,000 being reached in 1885. By 1896, however, business had once more fallen off. There was a sale recorded as low as $14,000. From then on, coincident with the consolidation period and the steady increase of national stock distribution, the rise in the value of a "seat" has been steady and precipitate. In the last week of 1901, a membership changed hands at $80,000. In 1909, still a new high was reached at $96,000, and by January, 1920, the record figure was $115,000. In 1928, a new member, before the increased membership proportionately reduced the quotation, was obliged to pay $600,000 for the privilege of trading on the floor of the New York Stock Exchange.

The absorption of the competitive trading organizations into the Stock Exchange membership did not for long eliminate other independent organizations. From time to time, new exchanges were formed, some on a substantial basis, and others designed only to serve as vehicles of manipulation for the interested sponsors. In the seventies, there were in existence an independent Mining Board and a Petroleum Board. The first of these had but a short life, for the public soon became aware of the fact that its securities depreciated in value as its officials were successful in distributing their holdings to their customers. When its sponsors had succeeded in getting rid of large amounts of worthless paper at inflated prices, the first Mining Board decided to liquidate and distribute its assets among the members. A fitting conclusion was the discovery that the treasurer had absconded with all the money belonging to the organization, and the organization came to an abrupt end without the necessity of formal liquidation. Later, a new Mining Board, under more substantial patronage, was inaugurated, but had only a short life. The hectic public speculation in gold during the Civil War resulted in the formation of independent gold exchanges, since this form of trading was not permitted on the "Big Board." The best known of these "outlaw" organizations was the "Coal Hole," so called because it held its meetings in a cellar. With the return of the greenbacks to par and the subsequent stabilization of currency quotations, these exchanges disappeared.

To-day there are two reputable national securities trading organizations in New York not connected with the New York Stock Exchange. The New York Curb Market, earning its name from the fact that for a long time its trading was conducted in the open air on Broad Street, has long served to make a market for those securities not yet seasoned for admission to the "Big Board." A few years ago, this growing body moved into a building of its own, and now acts as an efficient agency for securing a sufficient public distribution of new issues to permit of their admission later to listing on the "Big Board."

The New York Produce Exchange, using the name of this old commodity market, has in the last year converted its organization into a securities exchange. Its listings follow the type admitted to Curb dealings, but it has as yet not extensively developed its scope of activities. In about thirty cities of the United States there are local stock exchanges which are designed to make a market for securities of purely local interest or distribution.

To-day the New York Stock Exchange stands as the most important trading institution in the world. The value of its membership rights amounts to about $750,-

000,000, and under its supervision, billions of dollars of securities change hands every day. Under its own roof, it provides a mammoth clearing organization, loan facilities for its members, a separate bond department, a complete safe-deposit system, and a large and efficient auditing department, which in its stringent supervision, requires more rigid obedience to its doctrines than any governmental banking department. So effective has been this supervision, that in ten years, the average of business failures of members of the Exchange was less than one-half per cent per annum. This compares with a recent record of eight per cent for State banks in the United States.

The New York Stock Exchange, in theory only a voluntary association of brokers and dealers, is in fact the most powerful single exchange organization in the world. It wields immense power, and in spite of relentless efforts to bring it under the control of governmental bodies, operates and flourishes as an independent agency, making its own rules, settling all disputes among members, and revising its methods as changing conditions dictate. The Governing Committee exercises legislative, judicial, and executive power. A financial government within a political government, it maintains exclusive power over its subjects. Like the Pope, independent of Italy in his temporal lands, the Stock Exchange remains outside of the power of our political Government, although its activities touch as closely the

THE NEW YORK STOCK EXCHANGE TODAY

BOARD ROOM OF THE EXCHANGE

welfare of our investing body as do our banks and other financial organizations, all of which are closely watched and carefully supervised to guard the public's interest.

By its wisdom in effecting the purposes of governmental supervision by its own internal machinery, the New York Stock Exchange has justified its existence, earned and retained the confidence of the public, and proved itself the most reliable and efficient market place in the world. In this great mart are centered the activities of the younger men who are even now adding their fragments to the ever continuing story of Wall Street.

A NOTE ON THE BIBLIOGRAPHY

THE literature of Wall Street and its leaders is surprisingly meager. In political activities the dominant figures are often men of literary ability, and their memoirs, letters and autobiographies sometimes throw new light on secret activities. Leaders in finance and business are notoriously inarticulate, and until a few years ago what biographies were written were, in the main, the official, laudatory type of family memoir, of little help in adding to our knowledge of the men or their activities. In the last few years, much excellent work has been done along the lines of careful investigation into speculative history, and from old newspaper files, Government records and reports from personal acquaintances, some of the more recent workers in the field have been successful in unearthing facts which give a true picture of some of the leaders and their activities.

No effort is made here to list or record the many legislative inquiries and reports which have revealed much interesting material. Although our legislative bodies have seldom acted on any of these investigations, they have in an unforeseen way almost justified their work, for it is these legislative inquiries which present the student with the most reliable data. These reports make dull reading on the whole, but for the research worker in the field they now and then clearly illumine the basic facts of a transaction.

In 1879 James K. Medberry published a book called *Men and Mysteries of Wall Street*. This volume gives a readable account of the Street's activities at the time and a good description of the earlier operators. It is all taken from current stories, however, and may not be entirely accurate. About ten years earlier, Henry Adams and his brother Francis Adams, having little to occupy them at the time, came to New York and conducted a personal investigation into the speculative operations centering around the Erie Railroad. While Jay Gould refused to see them they were successful in interviewing Jim Fisk and other leaders, and after persistent inquiry succeeded in rescuing the most pertinent facts concerning the earlier jugglings of the Erie. In 1868, they published *Chapters on the Erie*, a volume which even to-day furnishes by far the most exciting and accurate account of those hectic days. The volume is now unfortunately out of print, but many libraries still have copies on their shelves.

As each one of the leading figures retired or died, it became the custom, except in the few cases where the subject was articulate enough to write his own story, for the family to engage a professional writer to prepare a biography which would not outrage the sensibilities of the descendants. Thus we have:

E. H. Harriman, A Biography, by George Kennan (Boston, 1912).

The Life of James J. Hill, by Joseph J. Pyle (New York, 2 vols., 1917).

Jay Cooke, Financier of the Civil War, by E. P. Oberholtzer (Philadelphia, 2 vols., 1927).

J. P. Morgan, by Carl Hovey (New York, 1912).

These and other biographies of a similar nature are accurate in their names and dates, but the writers are apparently often too aware of the origin of their assignment. As a result, these biographies can not always be depended upon to give a complete and unbiased account of any transaction.

Of the very few autobiographies or memoirs which have come from the pens of the great of Wall Street, only one requires comment. Henry Clews, first in *Twenty-Eight Years in Wall Street* and later in his enlarged *Fifty Years in Wall Street,* has given us an interesting, if not well organized account of his activities and associations. Most of the volume is taken up with his own work, but that part which is not is well worth reading as a first-hand story of some of Wall Street's high lights.

Coming down to more recent times, we find an increasing number of accurate accounts, interestingly written and presented in an organized fashion. In 1905, the New York Stock Exchange engaged the famous poet and banker, Clarence Edmund Stedman, to prepare a history of that body. The result of Stedman's extensive research appears in *The New York Stock Exchange*, published in 1905. This book, privately printed and circulated and now available only through libraries, gives a brilliant recital of the development of the Stock Exchange and its facilities. Unbiased, clear, detailed and well written, it has served the present writer consistently in his account of the early days of the Exchange brokers. For the explanation of the actual mechanical operation of the Exchange, the best volume is probably J. Edward Meeker's *The Stock Exchange* (New York, 1922). Mr. Meeker is the economist of the New York Stock Exchange and a leading authority in the field.

The reader interested in a vivid account of the physical development of Wall Street will find *The Story of a Street* by Frederic Trevor Hill (New York, 1908) accurate and interesting.

Of individual figures, there have been in the last few years many very readable biographies published. A few years ago Bouck White published *The Book of Daniel Drew,* which purported to be Drew's life story as taken from his diary. This is open to question, but in any case the result is exceedingly good. While the conversation is probably manufactured the facts are correct, and the manner of relating them heightens the interest and amusement of the reader. Ida Tarbell in *The Standard Oil Company* has given us the definite account of the rise of that great organization. In *John D., A Study in Oils,* John K. Winkler (New York, 1929) has presented a clever portrait of the Oil King. This volume is not meaty, but with its intimate touch fills out the more scholarly book by Miss Tarbell. In 1927 Denis Tilden Lynch published his *"Boss" Tweed,* which incidentally covered some of the operations of the financial leaders who were Tweed's close associates. A. D. Howden Smith followed his *Commodore Vanderbilt,* published in 1928, by his biography, *John Jacob Astor,* in the following year. Both of these volumes are written in a sprightly, journalistic style which adds interest in the reading without detracting from the basic value of the material presented. In the same year, *Jay Gould, the Story of a Fortune,* was published by the present writer, followed by *Jubilee Jim,* a fictional account of the life of Jim Fisk, by Robert H. Fuller.

Many general accounts have covered the financial development of the country in a masterly way. One of these books is *The Age of Big Business* by Burton J. Hendrick (in the Chronicles of America, New Haven, 1904). Professor Arthur M. Schlesinger has given us an authoritative account in *A Political and Social History of the United States.* Pre-eminent among all this type of books, however, is a work which any person interested in the economic development of the country

A NOTE ON THE BIBLIOGRAPHY

will read with enthusiasm and profit. Written in a charming literary style, authoritative yet not dull, its brilliance reveals the basic facts in every stage of our social and economic progress. This book is *The Rise of American Civilization* by Charles A. and Mary Beard (two volumes, New York, 1927).

THE END

INDEX

INDEX

[357]

INDEX

INDEX

INDEX

INDEX

INDEX